THE ARCHITECT AND SOCIETY
EDITED BY
JOHN FLEMING AND HUGH HONOUR

British Museum ground floor plan
(schematic: not to scale)

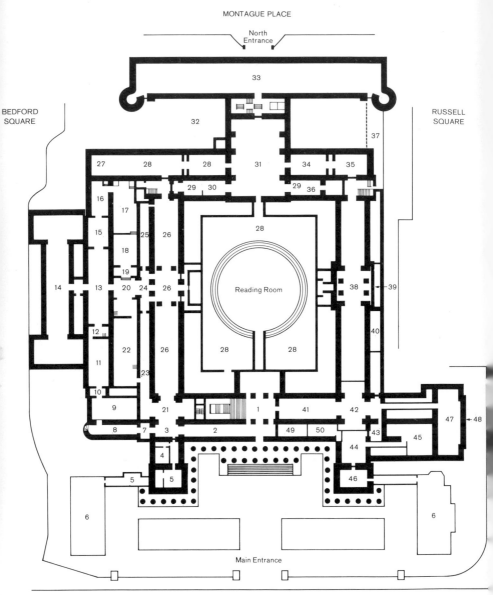

MONTAGUE PLACE

North
Entrance

BEDFORD
SQUARE

RUSSELL
SQUARE

33

32

37

27 28 28 31 34 35

29 30 29 36

16 28

17

15 25 26 28

18

19 Reading Room

14 13 20 24 26 38 39

12 40

11 22 26 28 28

23

10

9 21 1 41 42 47 48

8 7 3 2 49 50 43 45

4 44

5 46

5

6 6

Main Entrance

GREAT RUSSELL STREET

THE BRITISH MUSEUM

J. MORDAUNT CROOK

ALLEN LANE THE PENGUIN PRESS

Allen Lane The Penguin Press
74 Grosvenor Street, London W1

ISBN 0 7139 0254 X

Printed in Great Britain by
W & J Mackay Limited, Chatham
Set in Monophoto Garamond
Designed by Gerald Cinamon

TO MARGARET

Contents

Acknowledgements

Illustrations are reproduced by permission of: Mansell Collection, 1, 2; Warburg Institute, 3, 51, 52, 55, 61, 62, 66, 82; Courtauld Institute, 5, 6; Royal Academy, 7; Vatican Museum, 8; National Portrait Gallery, 11, 12, 68; British Museum, 13, 14, 16, 18–23, 26, 27, 45, 47, 50, 64, 67, 71, 73–6, 78, 81, 84; Royal Institute of British Architects, 17, 43, 53, 54, 56, 85, 92, 95; Bodleian Library, 25; National Monuments Record, 29, 32, 36, 37, 38; Scottish National Monuments Record, 31, 34; Royal Commission on Historical Monuments, 35; Country Life Ltd, 39, 77; Staatsbibliothek, Munich, 42; U.S. Information Service, 86; Public Record Office, 93, 94.

Photographs are reproduced by permission of: Günther Becker, Cassel, 9; Eric de Maré, 10, 30, 33, 58, 65, 89, 90, 91, 96, 99, 100; F. Jewell Harrison, 15; John R. Freeman, 24, 59, 60, 63, 79; Nicolas Cooper, 28; A. F. Kersting, 40; F. Kaufmann, 41; Thomas Photos, Oxford, 69; Mrs M. Warner, 80; Fox Photos, 83; Chevojon, 87; Mann Brothers, 97; Mr A. B. Waters, 98.

Illustrations 4 and 57 are reproduced by kind permission of H.M. The Queen; 46, 48, 49 are from author's collection; the schematic plan of the British Museum and 44 were redrawn by Paul White.

Copyright material in Chapter 4 is reproduced by permission of the Controller of H.M. Stationery Office.

Illustrations

21. Design for the Townley Gallery in the style of Montagu House (1803), G. Saunders.
22. Design for the Townley Gallery (1803), G. Saunders.
23. Design for the Townley Gallery, cross section (1803), G. Saunders.
24. The Townley Gallery, interior, G. Saunders. From R. Ackermann, *Repository of the Arts* (1810).
25. The Townley Gallery: arrangement of exhibits.
26. *Sir Robert Smirke*, 1828. Bust by E. H. Baily.
27. Covent Garden Theatre, London (1808-9), Sir Robert Smirke. From R. Ackermann, *Repository of the Arts* (1809).
28. The Old Council House, Bristol (1824-7), Sir Robert Smirke.
29. The Royal College of Physicians (now part of Canada House), London (1822-5), Sir Robert Smirke.
30. Sir John Soane's Museum, London.
31. The Hunterian Museum, Glasgow (1804), William Stark. Demolished 1865.
32. City Art Gallery, Manchester (1823), Sir Charles Barry.
33. Ashmolean Museum, Oxford (1841-5), C. R. Cockerell.
34. Royal Scottish Academy (1822-6 and 1832-5), W. H. Playfair.
35. Fitzwilliam Museum, Cambridge (1837-75), George Basevi.
36. Harris Free Library, Museum and Art Gallery, Preston (1882-93), J. Hibbert.
37. National Gallery, London (1832-8), William Wilkins.
38. Tate Gallery, London (1897), Sydney Smith.
39. Normanby Park, Lincolnshire (1821), Sir Robert Smirke.
40. The British Museum (1823), Sir Robert Smirke.
41. The Glyptothek, Munich (1816-30), Leo von Klenze.
42. The Altes Museum, Berlin (designed 1823, built 1825-8), K. F. Schinkel.
43. Grand Prix Design for a Museum (1779), François Jacques Delannoy.
44. Ground plan of the Parliament House, Dublin, Sir Edward Lovett Pearce.
45. The Parliament House, Dublin (1729 onwards), Sir Edward Lovett Pearce. From J. Malton, *A Picturesque and Descriptive View of the City of Dublin* (1792-9).
46. Smirke's final design for the British Museum. Lithograph by A. Mackenzie (1844).
47. Ground plan of the British Museum (1827), Sir Robert Smirke.
48. Design for the interior of the quadrangle of the British Museum (1823), Sir Robert Smirke.
49. Smirke's first design for the British Museum (1823).

Introduction

Architects have always been worldly men. Once they were courtiers and now they are communicators. Unlike painters or musicians, their work can never be created *in vacuo*. A building is the product not only of the man who designs it, but of the society which pays for it, lives in it and looks at it. So when we start to analyse a purpose-built public building like the British Museum we soon find ourselves involved as much with its purpose and its public as with its building. The British Museum has taxed the ingenuity of a score of architects – three of them R.I.B.A. Gold Medallists – over a period of two and a quarter centuries. Each made his own personal contribution. But each in turn found himself controlled and guided, inspired and exasperated, by the very nature of the institution he was trying to house. The institution made the building, as the turtle makes its shell. This book, therefore, attempts to explain the relationship between the British Museum as an institution and the British Museum as a piece of architecture. It is really a case study in aesthetic politics, an illustration of a much broader relationship, perenially troubled and perenially fruitful: the partnership of Architect and Society.

The full history of the British Museum has never been written. Perhaps it never will be. To trace, in detail, the development of each department – its acquisitions, its administration, its buildings, its personnel – would be an enormous job. No such attempt is made here. This is an essay in architectural history. But it does try to treat architectural history as more than stylistic analysis. Perhaps the background is sometimes allowed to dominate the building in the forefront of the picture. But an attempt has been made to keep the background in focus: to remind us that there is more to architectural history than motif-mongering.

There is also more to architectural history than the dissection of individual masterpieces. The British Museum is not a masterpiece. But at one time it was the largest secular building in the capital city of the most powerful country in the world. It is still the largest classical building in the British Isles – a national monument housing an institution with an international reputation. Topographers can hardly ignore it. And historians must do their best to explain its existence.

Then there is the personal side. The very fabric of our national museum seems to be encrusted with anecdotes. Some of them relate to the great and famous: Keats contemplating the Elgin Marbles; Karl Marx reading in the Round Room; Macaulay at his table in the King's Library; Carlyle complaining of a headache; Colin Wilson with his sleeping bag; Baron Corvo taking baths in the cloakroom. Other stories are happily anonymous. Every visitor has his favourite. And any book about the British Museum must include at least a few of them. My own fondest memory concerns a shabby man, wearily climbing the steps towards the haven of the Round Reading Room. As he slouched beneath the portico he reverently kissed the columns of the colonnade.

Several scholars – including of course both my kind editors – helpfully read this book in typescript, among them Sir John Summerson, Mr Howard Colvin and Dr Caroline Barron. I am most grateful for their advice. Finally, when time was short and spirits flagged, Cecil Kerr meticulously read the proofs and compiled the Index.

J.M.C.

The British Museum

1. The Treasury of the Athenians at Delphi (5th century B.C.)

1: The Idea of a Museum

'Man without learning, and the remembrance of thinges past,
falls into a beastlye sottishness' (Anon. 1653)

The Nine Muses ranked high among the daughters of Zeus. Born in Pieria at the foot of Mount Olympus, their favourite haunts were the grotto on Mount Helicon and the sacred well of Hippocrene. They sang at the banquets of the gods and, in return for libations of milk and honey, they revealed to mortals the magic of the arts and the mysteries of science. Their mother was Mnemosyne, goddess of memory, and though all nine bore different names, they were sometimes simply known as the Remembrances. 'Mind', 'muse' and 'memory' can all be linked – etymologically as well as conceptually. In appealing to the muses for inspiration, the poets, musicians and artists of ancient Greece were drawing upon the collective memory of their own society, disguised as the eternal wisdom of the gods. So it happened that the Greek μουσεῖον (mouseion) became first a shrine of the muses, then a repository for gifts, then a temple of the arts, and finally a collection of tangible memorials to mankind's creative genius.

Such was the classical idea of a museum. Its genesis has been traced back at least to the fifth century B.C., to the Treasury of the Athenians at Delphi [1] and the Pinakotheke, or picture gallery, in the Propylaea on the Acropolis at Athens. But its climax occurred two centuries later during the Hellenistic period, in the rival collections of Eumenes II at Pergamum and Ptolemy Philadelphus at Alexandria. Both were composite foundations. Here were libraries, collections of paintings and sculpture, and colleges for resident scholars – men like Zenodotus the Homeric critic and Callimachus the poet. Even in the dawn of recorded history, at Ur of the Chaldees, libraries and museums in primitive form were linked as centres of learning and inspiration – only a fragmented society would dream of separating them.

In the true sense of the Greek 'encyclopedia' – a complete circle of learning – Pergamum and Alexandria were never equalled in the ancient world. Yet they were eclipsed by the sheer quantity of works of art accumulated in ancient Rome. Enriched by the plunder of three continents, Rome itself became a gigantic treasure house. Seneca remarked that a private library had become as fashionable as a private bath. Unlike the Greek μουσεῖον, the Roman *museum* was frequently a private collection – Hadrian's villa at Tivoli [2], for example. 'What do you suppose', asked Cicero, 'has become of the wealth of the foreign nations who are now so poor, when you see Athens, Pergamum, Cyzicus, Miletus, Samos – nay, all Asia and Achaea, all Greece and Sicily, concentrated in these few houses?' But civic pride was almost as powerful a cultural

2. Hadrian's villa at Tivoli (2nd century A.D.)

impetus as private avarice. Roman libraries were frequently turned over to public use. Plutarch tells us that the Library of Lucullus 'was open to all. The Greeks who were at Rome resorted thither, as it were to the retreat of the Muses.' Augustus set up public libraries in the Temple of Apollo on the Palatine and in the Portico of Octavia in the Campus Martius. He also rebuilt the Temple of Concord to proclaim in sculpture and painting the eternal values of peace. And in the Baths of Titus or the Baths of Caracalla the Roman citizen enjoyed not only physical recreation but the aesthetic therapy of works of art. In the Baths of Diocletian there was a library as well. Long before that, however, the classical, comprehensive idea of a museum had already been summed up when Rameses II of Egypt inscribed over the doorway of his library at Thebes the simple legend: 'a place of healing for the soul.'

The modern museum has therefore a long classical ancestry. But as an institution, secular and public, it really stems from a Neo-classical idea, and dates only from the eighteenth century. Almost by definition, classical and Neo-classical share some of the same spiritual premises. But between these two phases in the long history of museology lie the Middle Ages and the Renaissance. And both those epochs, in very different ways, helped to shape the character of the modern museum.

The monastic library naturally occupies a key position in the history of medieval civilization. St Benedict of Aniane has some claim to be regarded as the librarian's patron saint. Less obvious, perhaps, is the role of the monasteries as custodians of works of art. The modern museum is a place of secular inspiration. Medieval churches were also museums, but museums of the spirit, visualizing religious experience in artistic form. Collections of holy books, vessels and images were kept in the earliest Christian churches. St Augustine pleaded in vain that 'God's holy temple is marvellous, not in pillars, marbles and in gilded ceilings, but in righteousness'. Yet valuables and curiosities continued to accumulate in monastic reliquaries and cathedral treasuries, from the trophies of Charlemagne to the treasures of Saint Louis, from Durham

to Rheims, from the Sainte-Chapelle in Paris to St Mark's in Venice. Abbot Suger's twelfth-century inventory of treasures in the Royal Abbey of St Denis concludes with an explanation: 'we urge that they be laid out . . . in order to propitiate the supreme power of Divine Majesty and to enhance the devotion of the brethren.' Durandus, liturgist and symbolist, took a similar line: 'in our churches two eggs of ostriches and other things of like kind, which cause admiration and which are rarely seen, are accustomed to be suspended, that by their means the people may be drawn to church, and have their minds the more affected.' In the church at Wittenburg on whose doors Luther nailed his theses, two whale ribs were exhibited: they were said to come from the Holy Land, but in fact were salvaged from a whale washed up on the shores of the Baltic. In much the same way the skins of gorillas, brought from the west coast of Africa by the navigator Hanno, had been hung up in the temple at Carthage. The *Heiltumsbuch* of 1510 itemized the narrative mosaics, the precious fabrics, jewels and exquisite treasures of St Mark's, Venice. But when Montfaucon reported in 1725 he seems to have been equally interested in a pair of unicorn's horns . . . and 'they show you likewise a lilly, offer'd by Henry III of France to the most Serene Republic, and a surprising pearl called mother-pearl, and several things of that nature'. In other words, collections of religious relics often become part of – and justification for – a hoard of miscellaneous curiosities. The heterogeneity of the seventeenth-century museum stems at least partly from this tradition of ecclesiastical miscellanies – a tradition which survived into the eighteenth century and later in the form of monastic collections, as at Melk and Seitenstetten in Austria. Secular accumulations of *objets d'art* in the late medieval period – notably that of Jean, Duke of Berry (1340–1416), brother of Charles V of France – were similarly amorphous, and also anticipated, in their variety at least, the princely collections of the Renaissance.

The transition from the medieval 'treasury' to the Renaissance *museo* involved a museological revolution. Medieval museums existed to express the eternal, not to explain the past. By turning inwards upon man and his achievements, the Renaissance made possible the admiration of works of art for their own sake rather than as reflections of divine omniscience. Hence the development of the great Renaissance collections, such as those of the Medici in Florence, the Este in Ferrara and the Montefeltro of Urbino and Gubbio. These were all prestige collections, along the lines of the *museo* of Lorenzo the Magnificent (d. 1492) in Florence. But the humanistic impulse also created a new interest in natural history: there were said to be 250 natural history museums in sixteenth-century Italy, most notably that of the Neapolitan chemist Ferrante Imperato [3]. The diversity of Renaissance scholarship eventually produced several remarkable historical and scientific collections: the portrait museum of Paolo Giovio (1443–1552) in Como, for example, and the scientific museums of Ulisse Aldrovandri (1522–

3. The museum of Ferrante Imperato, Naples in 1599

1605) in Bologna and Ole Worm (1588–1654) in Copenhagen. But of course it was in Rome that the Renaissance *museo* reached its apotheosis. Sixtus IV founded the Museo Capitolino; Julius II turned the Gardens and Cortile of the Belvedere into an open-air museum; and Leo X appointed Raphael superintendent of the Capitoline and Vatican museums.

In Rome the world of the Renaissance and its classical sources of inspiration were most obviously and tangibly linked. Elsewhere in Europe the contrast between medieval and Renaissance attitudes to the past were perhaps rather more striking. The Renaissance approach to works of art and scientific specimens introduced a crucial element into the development of the modern museum: a sense of historical perspective. This new faculty, only dimly visible in the medieval world, emancipated exhibits from an overall religious-cum-magical context by breaking the cyclical time-scale of medieval metaphysics. The endless rhythms of season and liturgy, of astronomy and astrology, gave way to a sense of historical progression – the basis of museology as a science. In the words of Germain Bazin, a museum is 'a temple where time seems suspended'. That is, each exhibit exists in its own temporal context. In the long run this new attitude produced its own architectural expression: an independent building designed specifically to house and display books, works of art and natural history specimens. Such a building does not in fact appear until the end of the seventeenth century. And only the triumph of historicism in the Neo-classical period brought the idea of a museum to fruition. Still, the genesis of the museum can be discerned in the sixteenth and early seventeenth centuries in the development of two subordinate building-types: the cabinet and the gallery.

The Italian *gabinetto*, the French *cabinet*, the English *closet*, the German *Kammer* or *Kabinett*, were all varieties of the same thing: a small room for displaying curiosities, *objets d'art*, books and lesser pictures, arranged regardless of interior decoration, the collection itself forming the decorative scheme. The German genius for verbal gymnastics evolved a whole range of minor categories: *Raritätenkabinett* (rarities), *Kuriositäten-*

4. *The Tribuna of the Uffizi, Florence* (1772-9), J. Zoffany

kabinett (curiosities), *Naturalienkabinett* (natural history specimens), *Münzkabinett* (medals) and *Mineralienkabinett* (minerals), among others. From 1563 onwards, at Castle Ambros near Innsbruck, the collection of Archduke Ferdinand of Tyrol (1529–95) included rooms labelled *Kunstkammer* (art), *Schatzkammer* (precious metals), *Wunderkammer* (natural curiosities) and *Rüstkammer* (armour). But the most famous example occurred in the Netherlands: Rubens's own cabinet of paintings, busts and medallions arranged in an apsidal saloon.

By contrast the gallery was a long room for the display of books, large paintings and sculptures, in which works of art formed an integral part of the decoration. Deriving from the *grande salle* of French medieval châteaux, the gallery emerged in museological form in Italy towards the end of the sixteenth century. The architectural writer Serlio (1475–1554) produced a prototype gallery plan. Bramante's galleries connecting the Vatican with Innocent VIII's Belvedere, date from *c.* 1510; Fontana's great gallery in the adjacent Vatican Library was built by Sixtus V in 1587. Buontalenti's east wing and Tribune at the Uffizi [4] in Florence were added about 1581. But more important than all these is the gallery at Sabbioneta near Mantua, built by Vespasiano Gonzaga *c.* 1560 as an 'antiquarium' to contain his collection of antique statues and reliefs. It is perhaps the oldest gallery still in use constructed specifically as a museum. During the seventeenth and early eighteenth centuries the gallery reached its culmination: the grande galerie at the Louvre (1610) [5–6], the Hall of Mirrors at Versailles (1678), and the Galleria Colonna (opened 1703) and Galleria Corsini (1729) in Rome. It was the combination of gallery and cabinet which produced the architectural formation of the modern museum. But another ingredient was also required: open access to the public. And this ingredient was a product not of the Renaissance but of the Enlightenment.

Most of the great seventeenth-century collections – those of Richelieu, Mazarin or Jabach for example – were occasionally available for public inspection. Mazarin's library was open to the public each Thursday from eight to eleven in the morning and from two to five in the afternoon. The Ambrosian Library at Milan, built by Cardinal Frederigo Borromeo between 1603 and 1609, formed part of a larger scheme including a college of doctors, a school of art, a museum and a botanic garden, all of which were open to the public. In early seventeenth-century London courtiers enjoyed Charles I's amazing art collection at Whitehall; sycophants affected to praise the Duke of Buckingham's treasures at York House; and savants revelled in the antique sculptures collected at Arundel House by Thomas Howard, Earl of Arundel, 'the father of English *virtu*'. In Spain, humble subjects might even penetrate that extraordinary combination of library, museum, monastery, palace, hospital and university, Philip II's Escorial. But such accessibility was

5. *The Grande Galerie of the Louvre* (1790), Hubert Robert

6. *The Grande Galerie in Ruins: a fantasy* (1796), Hubert Robert

only incidental: all these collections, like those of the Renaissance, were primarily expressions of private affluence or royal power. Hence the development of the cabinet and the gallery within the context of existing architectural forms. The Grande Galerie at the Louvre [5-6] began as a giant passageway connecting a town house (the Louvre) to a country house (the Tuileries). Both the Stallburg at Vienna (before 1684) and the Stallhof at Dresden (1722-5) were stables converted into art galleries – just as the Uffizi was, strictly speaking, the 'offices' attached to the Palazzo Vechio. And in England the Earl of Arundel's gallery, known to us only from Daniel Mytens's painting of *c*. 1618 [7], seems to have been simply an architectural extension to a private house. In the eighteenth century even newly-built palaces maintained this tradition: Frederick the Great's picture gallery at Sanssouci (1787) near Potsdam, for

7. *The Earl of Arundel in the Sculpture Gallery at Arundel House*
(*c.* 1618), D. Mytens

example. And the greatest of Neo-classical art galleries, the Museo Pio-Clementino [8], built to designs by Michelangelo Simonetti and Guiseppe Camporesi (c. 1773–86), was itself an extension to the Vatican.

The exhibition of works of art had therefore not yet been separated from private display. The opening to the public in 1734 of the Museo Capitolino in Rome certainly marked a step forward. But by reason of its origins that was a collection which still evoked the museums of the past. The Museum Fredericianum at Cassel (1769–79) [9], built for the Landgrave Frederick II by his 'premier architecte', Simon Louis du Ry, has been put forward as the first independent building designed and constructed specifically as a public museum. Its range was indeed varied – books, antiquities, waxworks and natural history specimens. Hassencamp noted approvingly in 1783, 'I cannot think of any collection to compete with it, except that of the British Museum.' But such a com-

8 *(opposite)*. The Museo Pio-Clementino, Rome (*c.* 1773-86),
M. Simonetti and G. Camporesi

9. The Museum Fredericianum, Cassel (1769-79), Simon Louis du Ry

parison is both revealing and misleading. For all its architectural
novelty, the Museum Fredericianum looked backwards rather than forward as an institution. Its very title betrayed its princely origins. In this
respect it was the exact opposite of the British Museum. At Cassel the
element of royal display was still strong: the prince's own study formed
the heart of the architectural complex. Such a layout recalled the assump-
tions of Renaissance kingship – whereas the future of the museum was
national and democratic. The development of museums in the eighteenth
and nineteenth centuries was very largely bound up with their transference from private to public hands. In fact the emergence of the modern
museum seems at times almost an index of royal decline. Although
architecturally trivial by comparison with Cassel, the Charleston
Museum in South Carolina, U.S.A., was perhaps a more significant
portent: it was founded in 1773, the year of the Boston Tea Party.

But whatever the political circumstances, the eighteenth century turned out to be a museological watershed in almost every country. In general terms, the modern museum is a product of Renaissance humanism, eighteenth-century Enlightenment and nineteenth-century democracy. And of these three stages – occurring principally in Italy, France and Britain respectively – perhaps the most dramatic was the museological revolution associated with the Age of Reason.

Some of the treasures accumulated by Louis XIV and Louis XV were intermittently displayed in the Palais du Luxembourg between 1750 and 1779 – to the public twice a week and to the students of the École Royale at almost any time. But that was no more than a concession. Throwing open the French royal collections was therefore high among the cultural objects of the Enlightenment. In 1747 La Font de Saint-Yenne produced the first of many pleas for the establishment of a royal museum in Paris – that was five years after Count Algarotti's abortive scheme for a royal museum at Dresden. Diderot's *Encyclopédie* (1751–65) included an article on the Louvre, urging the creation of a '*Musée central des Arts et des Sciences*', a cultural centre along Alexandrian lines with convenient access for the public and accommodation for learned societies – a veritable Temple of Art and Science. Here was an idea – a Temple of the Arts and Sciences, albeit a royal one – which satisfied the historicist impulses of Neo-classicism as well as the social aspirations of the Enlightenment.

It was the philosophy of Neo-classicism which, during the 1820s, finally dictated the form and nature of the new British Museum. As such, it demands separate treatment in a later chapter. At this point we must merely remember that Neo-classical attitudes were fairly general throughout Europe between the 1760s and the 1830s, and that perhaps the most persistent Neo-classical mirage was the creation of a national Temple of Art. It was a mirage which afflicted aesthetic pundits in most European countries. When in 1763 an anonymous English pamphleteer looked forward one hundred years to *The Reign of George VI*, he prophesied the setting up of a new capital city in the heart of Rutland, and inevitably included among its major monuments a royal palace which outshone all the libraries and art galleries of Europe: 'this glorious building was not only the residence of royalty, but might properly be called the Temple of the Muses.' When the French Academy of Architecture first offered their *Grand Prix* in 1779, the subject chosen for competition was, almost inevitably, 'A Museum'. Both prize-winners – Gisors and Delannoy – set out to cover a wide range of arts and sciences. Their plans included a botanical garden and library, a cabinet for medals, rooms for housing geographical exhibits and engravings, as well as halls for the display of the arts and natural history. Boullée, an architectural visionary, produced a similar museological fantasy in 1783.

In Austria and France, towards the end of the eighteenth century, the Temple emerged in rather more tangible form – with a firm pedagogical foundation. For a museum was regarded by the Enlightenment as at least partly a training ground for creative artists. In 1779 Christian von Mechel, a friend of Winckelmann, began to rearrange the Austrian Imperial collection in the Belvedere Museum, Vienna. 'The purpose', he wrote, 'was to use this beautiful building, so suitable by its separate rooms, so that the arrangement should be as far as possible a visible history of art. Such a large, public collection intended for instruction more than for fleeting pleasure, is like a rich library in which those eager to learn are glad to find works of art of all kinds and all periods.' In 1781 the Belvedere was largely opened to visitors, and by 1792 the collections were available on Monday, Wednesday and Friday, to anyone 'with clean shoes'. Christian von Mechel's utilitarian approach was paralleled, and eventually overtaken, by another aspect of the same enlightening impulse: the idea that a museum was a spiritually ennobling place. In 1778 Aloys Hirt remarked, in the context of the Prussian royal collection, that it was 'beneath the dignity of an ancient monument to be displayed as an ornament'. Works of art, he believed, should be kept not in palaces but in public museums. 'They are a heritage for the whole of mankind. . . . Only by making them public and uniting them in display can they become the object of true study; and every result obtained from this is a new gain for the common good of mankind.' This was Winckelmann's view: a passionate belief in the morally elevating effect of great works of art. In other words, the purpose of the Neo-classical museum was not only educational but inspirational. And the achievement of both purposes depended on the opening of museums to the widest possible public.

In this respect Paris was only slightly slower than Vienna. Under Louis XVI Count d'Angiviller's attempts to rationalize the display and classification of the royal treasures have come to be regarded as a milestone in the history of museum techniques. The royal collection in Paris might eventually have become a museum, like the royal collection in Vienna, with d'Angiviller playing the part of Christian von Mechel. The Louvre might have become as public as the Belvedere. But, like the Belvedere, it would still have been a royal collection. It required the Revolution to turn the idea of a museum into one of the basic institutions of the modern state. Between 1793 and 1816 under various names – Museum National, Museum Français, Musée Central, Musée Napoléon – the Louvre fulfilled the museological dreams of the Enlightenment. Enriched by the plunder of war and inspired by the learning and enthusiasm of two great curators, Denon and Lenoir, Paris became the museological centre of the world. France now had a museum which was neither private, nor royal, nor religious. The Musée Napoléon was open to the public, overtly secular and aggressively national. But all three characteristics – accessibility, secularity and nationality – had already been anticipated elsewhere: in England.

When Diderot produced his far from cyclopedic entry on museums, he specifically mentioned the name of only one: the Ashmolean Museum at Oxford [10]. Such emphasis was perfectly justifiable, for in many ways the Ashmolean was the first modern museum. It was certainly the first great museological institution specifically designed for exhibition purposes, open to the public and organized on a pedagogical basis. By comparison the Wasserkirche at Zurich (1629) and the university museum

10. The Old Ashmolean Museum, Oxford (1679-83), Thomas Wood

at Basle (1661) were merely straws in the wind. In England there were scarcely any precedents, except perhaps the establishment in 1602 of the gallery of antiquities in the Bodleian Library, and the opening in 1670 of the Armouries in the Tower of London. The Ashmolean was a rather more ambitious venture. Founded by an inveterate traveller and naturalist, John Tradescant the Elder (d. 1638), the Ashmolean collection passed – after some protracted legal squabbles – via John Tradescant the Younger (1608-62) to Elias Ashmole (1617-92), 'the greatest virtuoso and curioso that ever was known or read of in England before his time', and thence in 1675 to Oxford University. The Tradescant collection had originally been housed in South Lambeth. Ashmole added to it many items of his own and bequeathed the whole collection to his old university. Thus 'the name of Tradescant was unjustly sunk in that of Ashmole'.

Unlike the collections of paintings and sculpture built up earlier in the seventeenth century by Charles I, Buckingham and Arundel, the scope and contents of the first Ashmolean Museum belonged to the heterogeneous tradition of the cabinet. The original collection was appropriately known by a variety of nicknames: 'Tradescant's Ark', Tradescant's 'Closet of Rarities', Tradescant's 'Closet of Curiosities'. In fact its chaotic variety made it directly comparable to several contemporary collections of oddities, such as those built up by Buffon in Paris, by Christian V of Denmark, or by Dr Albert Seba of Amsterdam – the latter bought by Peter the Great for his own collection in 1716. The development of scientific studies in the late seventeenth century was a serious business. But the contents of these collections read curiously today. Sir Thomas Browne's *Musaeum Clausum* (1686) nicely satirizes such hoards of

remarkable Books, Antiquities, Pictures and Rarities of several kinds scarce or never seen by any man now living. . . . Certain ancient Medals with Greek and Roman inscriptions found about Crim Tartary; conceived to be left in those parts by the Souldiers of *Mithradates*. . . . Ancient Ivory and Copper Crosses found with many others in *China*; conceived to have been brought and left there by the Greek Souldiers who served under Tamerlaine. . . . The Skin of a Snake bred out of the Spinal Marrow of a Man; Vegetable Horns mentioned by Linschoten which set in the ground grow up like Plants about Goa; Spirits and Salts of Sargasso made in the Western Ocean covered with that Vegetable; excellent against the Scurvy . . .

All this was not too far removed from what the poet Cleveland called Tradescant's 'Ark of novelties'. Its first catalogue, *Musaeum Tradescantianum* (1656) actually included items like 'the blood that rained in the Isle of Wight, attested by Sir John Oglander, a Dodo bird [its head and paw were saved from burning in 1755 and still survive in the University Science Museum], and a Bird sitting upon a perch natural, together with several drafts and pieces of painting of sundry excellent masters'. Under the heading 'Some Kindes of Birds, their Egges, Beaks, Feathers, Clawes and Spurres', we find 'Divers sorts of Egges from Turkie, one given for a Dragon's Egge. . . . Easter Eggs of the Patriarch of Jerusalem. . . . Two Feathers of the Phoenix Tayle. . . . The Claw of the bird Rock, who, as Authors report, is able to trusse an Elephant.' Under the headings 'Garments, Vestures, Habits and Ornaments' and 'Mechanick, Artificial Workes in Carvings, Turnings, Sawings and Paintings', we find Edward the Confessor's knitted gloves, the famous 'Pakotan, King of Virginia's habit, all embroidered with shells or Roanoke' – which still survives – and a 'Cherry-stone, upon one side S. George and the Dragon, perfectly cut, and on the other side 88 Emperours' faces'. No wonder Anthony Wood was reduced to describing Oxford's new acquisition as simply 'twelve cart loads of rarities'. The Scientific Revolution of the seventeenth century had replaced the miraculous by the curious.

The Ashmolean Museum was therefore a Cabinet of Curiosities *par excellence*. But in architectural arrangement its new building was really a series of minor galleries. Designed by the Oxfordshire master mason Thomas Wood, the layout of the new museum may well have been inspired by Sir Christopher Wren's unexecuted scheme for rehousing the

Royal Society in London. Constructed between 1679 and 1683, its three stories contained not only a series of apartments devoted to antiquities, natural history specimens and curiosities, but also a chemical laboratory, a lecture room and a library. Curators were chosen from the various Oxford colleges, and graduated admission fees were charged. For almost two centuries it remained the chief centre for scientific studies in the university, and the number and variety of exhibits continued to increase. Only in the late Victorian period were the natural history sections transferred to the University Science Museum (1860), and the ethnographical specimens to the Pitt Rivers Museum (1886). This method of consolidation and dispersal had already been adopted with regard to books, medals, paintings and sculptures: the new Ashmolean galleries, designed by C. R. Cockerell, were constructed in 1841-5 and have since been extended in 1894, 1908 and 1967. Stripped of the majority of its first possessions, the original Ashmolean building became, in 1925, a Museum of the History of Science.

In its accessibility, its comprehensive range and its educative purpose – as well as in its kaleidoscopic arrangement – the Ashmolean anticipated the British Museum. And the history of both institutions exhibits the same heterogeneous origins, followed by the same cyclical process of accumulation and fragmentation. But the scale of these two foundations was of course very different. By comparison with the British Museum the Ashmolean, for all its interest, was merely a museological microcosm. For when it was founded in 1753 the British Museum was the first museum in the world which was public, secular – and national.

2 : The Old British Museum

'Whereas, all arts and sciences have a connection with each other, and discoveries in natural philosophy, and other branches of speculative knowledge . . . do and may . . . give help and success to the most useful experiments and inventions; therefore . . . not only for the inspection and entertainment of the learned and the curious, but for the general use and benefit of the public; may . . . it be enacted . . .that within . . . London or Westminster . . . one general repository shall be erected . . .for public use to all posterity.' ('An Act to incorporate the British Museum', 1753)

The British Museum had three founders: Sir Robert Cotton (1570–1631), Robert Harley, Earl of Oxford (1661–1724) and Sir Hans Sloane (1660–1753). Or rather, the possessions of these three men constituted the three foundation collections. The real founder of the British Museum was the House of Commons.

11. *Sir Robert Cotton* (1570–1631), Artist unknown.
Copy after C. Johnson

12. *Robert Harley, 1st Earl of Oxford* (1661–1724),
Artist unknown. Copy after Kneller

39

Sir Robert Cotton [11], that 'magazine of history', that artful 'ingros-ser of antiquities', 'that most industrious collector' – to quote only three contemporary descriptions – accumulated the finest collection of medi-eval manuscripts in Britain. His political career was hardly illustrious: he made use of his friendship with James I to build up a priceless hoard of state papers which he then allowed to be used as precedents for Parliamentary attacks on Charles I. On the whole he is better remem-bered as a collector and a friend of Camden and Ben Jonson. The Lindisfarne Gospels, the Anglo-Saxon Chronicle, Magna Carta, several Saxon charters – these were just a few of his treasures. Louis XIV is said to have offered £60,000 for them, plus the award of any French title which Cotton's grandson cared to name. However, in accordance with its founder's wishes, the Cottonian Library was belatedly made over to the English state by Act of Parliament in 1700, 'for public use and advantage'. Elkanah Settle wrote a turgid poem called *'Minerva Trium-phant'*, and Sir Christopher Wren was commissioned to design an appropriate depository. A triple foundation was envisaged: the Cotton collection, the Gresham College collection and the Queen's library at St James's Palace. But the scheme came to nothing.

This was not the first time that a national or central public Library had been proposed. In 1555 the astrologer John Dee had begged 'Bloody' Mary to make up for her father's dissolution of the monasteries by creating a royal library of manuscripts. Soon afterwards Archbishop Parker and the explorer Humphrey Gilbert, fellows of the first Society of Antiquaries, tried to set up a public library called The Library of Queen Elizabeth, after the pattern set by 'the more civilised nations as Germany, Italy and France', who 'take care to encourage learning by Public Lectures, Libraries and Academies'. In the 1680s John Evelyn wished to create a public library in part of St Paul's Cathedral – a scheme revived in the early eighteenth century by John Anstis, Garter King-of-Arms. All these ideas failed to materialize. So did two similar projects in 1697 and 1707: Richard Bentley's scheme for a 'Free Library' in 'a corner of St James's Park', based on the royal collection, subsidized by Parliamentary grants, and adorned with 'marbles . . . ancient inscriptions, basso-relievos etc. . . . from the African coast and Greece, and Asia the Less'; and Sir Hans Sloane's project for a public library in London based on the Cottonian Library, the Royal Library and the Library of the Society of Antiquaries.

Instead of being preserved in a national library designed by Wren, Sir Robert Cotton's collection was left to moulder away slowly – at Cotton House, Westminster (next to the House of Commons), at Essex House in the Strand, and at Ashburnham House, next to Westminster School, where it was partly destroyed by fire in 1731. At this point the House of Commons seems belatedly to have woken up to the value of the collection. Various attempts were made at classification and restoration. A Major Arthur Edwards added to it his own library and generously endowed it in his will. An historian, Thomas Carter, wished to make it generally available in the Mansion House, recently built to designs by George Dance the Elder (d. 1768). And when in 1753 the collections of Sir Hans Sloane at last came on the market, Arthur Onslow, the Commons' Speaker for thirty-three years, decided it was time to create some sort of national museum. He had in mind the conjunction of the Cottonian Library, the Sloane Museum and a third collection, the Harleian Library.

Robert Harley [12], 1st Earl of Oxford and Tory leader under Queen Anne, collected books and manuscripts in the grand manner. Unlike Cotton, he was a patron rather than a scholar: he specialized in fine bindings. Macaulay, who loathed his politics, called him 'a dull puzzle-headed man', having 'that sort of industry and that sort of exactness which would have made him a respectable antiquary or King-at-Arms'. Still, he had the good sense to employ a model librarian, Humphrey Wanley; and he was himself a Trustee of the Cottonian Library. By 1721 he owned twenty thousand books, six thousand volumes of manuscripts, fourteen thousand charters and five hundred rolls, including many items from the libraries of John Foxe, John Stow and Sir Symonds

D'Ewes. His son, Edward Harley the 2nd Earl, greatly added to the collection: when he died in 1741 there were eight thousand volumes of manuscripts, fifty thousand printed books, four hundred thousand pamphlets and forty thousand prints, besides coins, medals and portraits. By 1753 all but the manuscripts had been privately sold, and it was therefore only a portion – but the most valuable portion – of the Harleian Library which the House of Commons set out to buy. The dowager Countess of Oxford left the negotiations to her daughter, the Duchess of Portland. Onslow had suggested, via James West, an antiquarian M.P., the sum of £10,000. The price was ridiculously low. But the Duchess accepted. 'I will not', she told Onslow, 'bargain with the public.' So the Harleian manuscripts were purchased by Parliament as a suitable complement to the Cottonian Library. But neither collection would have formed part of the British Museum had it not been for the wisdom and foresight of the greatest collector in eighteenth-century England – Sir Hans Sloane [13], physician, naturalist and traveller.

Sloane's private museum began as a collection of botanical specimens which he brought back from France and the West Indies. John Evelyn noted in his *Diary* for 16 April 1691:

I went to see Dr Sloane's curiosities, being an universal collection of the natural productions of Jamaica, consisting of plants, fruits, corals, minerals, stones, earth, shells, animals and insects, collected with great judgment; several folios of dried plants, and one which had about eighty, several sorts of ferns, and another of grasses; the Jamaican pepper, in branch, leaves, flower, fruit etc.

This botanical collection eventually grew into the Sloane Herbarium, which now fills three hundred and thirty-seven large folio volumes in the Department of Botany in the Natural History section of the British Museum. Together with his collections of zoological specimens, shells, insects, fossils and minerals it soon came to be regarded as the finest natural history collection in the world. Besides this, Sloane accumulated classical, medieval and oriental antiquities, as well as coins, and medals,

13. *Sir Hans Sloane* (1660–1753),
a terra-cotta model by J. M. Rysbrack

drawings and paintings, books, pamphlets and manuscripts *en masse*. His library eventually exceeded forty thousand volumes, being particularly strong in medicine and natural history, his manuscripts alone totalling more than four thousand items. In 1725 he had some twenty thousand coins and medals; by 1752 he had thirty-two thousand. By 1753 his whole collection was reckoned as 'sixty-nine thousand, three hundred and fifty-two particulars, including the Manuscripts'. At his death in 1753 there were no less than 79,575 objects, *excluding* the plants in his herbarium. As regards books and antiquities, Sloane was perhaps surpassed by his contemporary, Dr Mead. But the total range and scope of his collection remained unrivalled.

Sloane's enormous collections were initially housed in his mansion in Great Russell Street, just off Bloomsbury Square – today No. 3, Bloomsbury Place. As his possessions grew more and more extensive he was obliged to buy up the house next door. His private museum became one of the sights of London. Several amusing stories are quoted by Sloane's biographer, Sir Gavin De Beer. Benjamin Franklin visited the great 'Lover of Curiosities' in 1725 and sold him an asbestos purse. Voltaire arrived in 1727, and Linnaeus in 1736. In 1740 the immortal Handel took tea in Sloane's library and outraged 'the poor old bookworm' by placing his buttered muffin on one of the rarer volumes.

Several visitors have left us detailed descriptions. In 1701 Ralph Thoresby called on

Dr Sloane in whose inestimable museum I was most courteously entertained many a pleasant hour: he has a noble library, two large rooms well stocked with valuable manuscripts and printed authors, an admirable collection of dried plants from Jamaica, the natural history of which he has in hand. . . . He gave me the printed catalogue of some Indian seeds: he has other curiosities without number, and above value; Bishop Nicholson (who is a competent judge, having been in those parts) says, it vastly exceeds those of many foreign potentates, which are so celebrated in history.

In 1710 it was the turn of a German scholar, Zacharias von Uffenbach. His account is worth quoting at length:

In the afternoon Herr Campe took us to Dr Hans Sloane, who received us very politely and in a manner greatly different from that of the coxcomb Dr Woodward [one of Sloane's rivals; founder of the Woodwardian medical museum at Cambridge]. He spoke to us at once in French, which, for an Englishman, is quite out of the ordinary. . . . He led us into four moderately large-sized rooms which were surrounded with filled cabinets. The tops are bookshelves arranged in three to four tiers, the cabinets below filled with natural history specimens. Here we found not only a great quantity of specimens but most of them are rare or unique. It contains the whole of the Charleton collection [willed to Sloane in 1702], and also a great many objects which were partly brought back from the West Indies by Sloane himself, and others which he continually adds at great cost. He assured me that the Venetian Ambassador had offered him £15,000 for the Collections but that he declined the offer.

There are a great many specimens of various materials, some preserved in spirit, and others dry; different kinds of strange fishes, and a great many mineral specimens, figured stones, and a number of precious stones, some of them of large size and very valuable. He possesses also a considerable collection of insects . . .

After inspecting these collections, we saw many Indian and other foreign clothes and weapons etc.; also a variety of cloth which is supposed to grow on a tree, and the antlers of a deer, nearly of the same size as that of the specimen that we saw at Windsor. Dr Sloane shewed us also a small cabinet which contained about four hundred kinds of agate, a great many of which were carved. He believes them all to be natural, but I doubt that. Further on there was a cabinet with various vessels and other objects made of agate, and others made from different precious stones and materials. There was also a cabinet of coins of all metals together with other antiquities and carved stones, but we had not enough time to look at them properly.

We next saw a cabinet of skins, some of them of birds together with nests of most unusual structure . . .

When we had seen as many of these things as time permitted, Dr Sloane asked us into another room where we sat at a table and had coffee, and Dr Sloane shewed us some rare books. There were a number of large books illustrated with paintings made from life of foreign animals, birds, herbs, flowers, shells etc.; and a special volume containing the costumes of various nations. The paintings were collected one by one from all parts of the world by Dr Sloane himself on his extensive travels, regardless of cost. Some of them are painted by famous painters . . . Lastly Dr Sloane shewed us some manuscripts, mostly of medical interest which were of recent times. The most outstanding of these was a description of the West Indian coast, very well done and written in Portuguese.

We were very sorry that this large and wonderful collection had to be seen in such a comparatively short time, but he has very little leisure because of his medical practice. It is said that an hour of his time is worth a guinea. Therefore we must take it as a great honour that he gave us from 2.30 to 7. He is very affable and pleasant despite having travelled so extensively, particularly civil to persons who have some scientific knowledge of his collection.

This, then, was Sloane's collection: the chief foundation of the future British Museum. Eighteenth-century wits and jokers found the whole thing an easy target: Hervey's 'stupid Sloane'; Pope's 'books for Mead and butterflies for Sloane'; Hearne's 'dear Doctor' with his quaint 'knick knackatory'; and Edward Young's famous description of 'the foremost toyman of his time' . . .

> How his eyes languish! how his thoughts adore,
> The painted coat that Joseph never wore.
> He shows, on holidays, a sacred pin
> That touched the ruff that touched Queen Bess's chin . . .
> Was ever year unblest as this, he'll cry
> It has not brought us one new butterfly?

At the age of eighty-one, Sloane decided to retire from Bloomsbury to his Manor House at Chelsea. His Quaker man-servant, Edward Howard, has left us a description of the agonizing process of removal during the spring of 1742: The Manor House

being very large, and capable to contain his library and all his collection of gimcracks, he left his house . . . near Bloomsbury Square, declined his practice of physic, and retired . . . with all his vast collection, all which, except a few which he used to bring himself in his chariot, passed through my hands. Those he brought himself were chiefly gold and silver medals, diamonds, jewels and other precious stones; and among these I doubt not but he had many gods of gold and gods of silver, for I one day unpacked a large case full of gods of the ancient Egyptians, Greeks and Romans etc. . . . He had forty volumes in folio – catalogues of his collection – and 42,000 other books in his library, among which was one room full of specimens of dried plants . . . He used to appoint the rooms in which the books were to be stored up, and I to receive them; they were sent loose in carts and tossed from the cart to a man on a ladder, who tossed them in at a window, up one pair of stairs, to a man who caught them there as men do bricks . . .

There, in Chelsea, among his 'curiosities', Sloane lived out his declining years, himself an object of curiosity, silent, deaf and confined to a three-wheeled bathchair. In June 1748, less than five years before his death, 'the good old gentleman . . . antient and infirm', received the Prince and Princess of Wales and showed them his treasures. Prince Frederick 'expressed the great pleasure it gave him to see so magnificent a collection in *England*', adding that 'it must conduce to the benefit of learning . . . to have it established for public use to the latest posterity'. For Sloane had long been determined that his life's work would not be broken up at his death. He planned to make it the nucleus of a major national collection.

Sloane's will, meticulously prepared in 1739 and modified in 1749 and 1751, made his intentions quite clear:

Desiring very much that . . . [my collections], tending many ways to the manifestation of the glory of God, the confutation of Atheism and its consequences, the use and improvement of physic, and other arts and sciences, and benefit of mankind, may remain together, and not . . . be separated, and that chiefly in and about the city of London . . . where they may by the great confluence of people be of most use . . . [I direct that they be offered to the King, for the nation, so that they] may be from time to time visited and seen by all persons desirous of seeing and viewing the same . . . [that they] . . . may be rendered as useful as possible, as well towards the satisfying the desire of the curious, as for the improvement of knowledge, and information of all purposes.

The purchase price was £20,000, to be paid to Sloane's two daughters. This was of course far below the collections' true value – Sloane once claimed they cost him £100,000. The offer was to be made in turn, on a two months' option, to the King, the Royal Society, Oxford University, the Edinburgh College of Physicians and the Royal Academies of Science in Paris, St Petersburg, Berlin and Madrid. Sloane nominated four executors and more than seventy trustees. One of them was Horace Walpole.

You will scarce guess [he wrote to Sir Horace Mann], how I employ my time; chiefly at present in the guardianship of embryos and cockle-shells. Sir Hans Sloane is dead and has made me one of the trustees to his museum, which is to be offered for twenty thousand pounds . . . he valued it at fourscore thousand; and so would anybody who loves hippopotamuses, sharks with one ear, and spiders as big as geese! It is a rent-charge to keep the foetuses in spirit! You may believe that those who think money the most valuable of all curiosities, will not be purchasers. The King has excused himself, saying he did not believe that there are twenty thousand pounds in the Treasury. We are a charming wise set, all philosophers, botanists, antiquarians, and mathematicians; and adjourned our first meeting, because Lord Macclesfield, our chairman, was engaged to a party for finding out the longitude . . .

Like his father, George II cared little for 'boetry and bainting'. As Pope put it, 'Dunce the Second reigns like Dunce the First'. So, the Crown having failed them, Sloane's Trustees petitioned the House of Commons. The Prime Minister, Henry Pelham, tried to 'throw cold water on the generous gift'. But Speaker Onslow, to his eternal credit, persuasively argued that here was a chance to unite Sloane's collection with those of Cotton and Harley. Here was a chance to form a national museum worthy of the name. A State Lottery was instituted to raise £300,000. A swindler named Peter Leheup made a fortune in black market tickets. But on the whole the idea worked well enough. Apart from £200,000 in prizes, £30,000 was to go to the Sloane and Harley families; £30,000 for salaries and expenses; and the remainder to provide 'a sufficient sum' for the construction or acquisition of a suitable building. Onslow said 'he was against Lotteries, but on this laudable occasion . . .' And on 7 June 1753, George II – a little unwillingly – assented to the Act of Parliament (26 Geo. II, *c.* 22) which created the British Museum. Four years later he made amends for his reluctance by formally presenting to the new museum the Old Royal Library, built up by successive Kings of England since the fifteenth century and lodged with the Cottonian Library since 1708. It comprised 12,000 volumes, including the priceless Codex Alexandrinus.

At last, the British Museum was founded. And these were the foundation collections – the product of two traditions, one historical, the other scientific: the antiquarianism of sixteenth- and seventeenth-century England, and the scientific curiosity of seventeenth- and eighteenth-century Europe. But where were all the exhibits to be housed? When Mrs Delaney heard about Sloane's will, she remarked how sad she would be to miss the fun of an auction, but added: 'I hope the King will . . . build a museum such as a King should have.' At least four architects were quick to seize the opportunity. Four rival designs were produced, one Rococo, and three Palladian.

Early in 1754 Cornelius Johnston, 'painter and architect', published a *Design for a British Museum or Public Repository and Cottonian Library* [14].

14. 'Design for a British Museum or Public Repository' (1754), Cornelius Johnston.

15. Design for a new British Museum (?1754), John Vardy

It was to be a sizeable quadrangular building, housing not only the Foundation Collections, but also the Royal and Antiquarian Societies, and a Royal Academy of painting, sculpture and architecture – in other words, a Temple of the Arts and Sciences. Moreover, it would have been a remarkable example of that most elusive of styles, the English Rococo. But no doubt the Trustees took fright at the cost. Instead, they appointed a committee to see whether William Kent's designs of the 1730s for rebuilding the Houses of Parliament could be disinterred and re-used for a British Museum. After all, Kent's plans had catered for the re-housing of the Cottonian Library. John Vardy (d. 1756), Kent's successor at the Office of Works, was directed to write a report. Naturally enough, he took the chance to produce his own set of designs [15] – and these were later exhibited at the Society of Artists in 1761. Very much in the tradition of Kent's Palladianism, they consisted of a domed central block flanked by wings containing domed rotundas. This Palladian vision of a British Museum would certainly have looked well in Whitehall. And perhaps Whitehall was indeed the site which Vardy was considering. For at about the same time John Gwynn (d. 1786), architect and town-planner, was dreaming of a British Museum within the ambience of Inigo Jones's Banqueting House and William Kent's Horse Guards. In 1771 he exhibited his scheme, retrospectively, at the Royal Academy. Another architect with the same dream was that 'Wizard of Durham', Thomas Wright (1711–86). But, like Johnston's effort, the projects by Gwynn and Vardy and Wright came to nothing. The British Museum was destined to be neither Rococo nor Palladian.

For the sake of economy, the Trustees decided to convert a building which already existed. By law the museum had to be 'one General Repository' – for 'all arts and sciences have a connection with each other'. It had, moreover, to remain 'for publick Use to all Posterity'. The building had, therefore, to be both solid and capacious. Sloane's Chelsea Manor House was felt to be too far from central London. Buckingham House – ancestor of Buckingham Palace – was considered. But the price,

£30,000, asked by the Duke of Buckingham was felt to be too high. So the choice fell upon Montagu House in Bloomsbury, a property of the Earl of Halifax, not far from Sloane's first private museum. The price was £10,250. Alterations – perhaps by Henry Keene (1726–76), a minor master in both Gothic and Classic – involved the rearrangement and subdivision of several rooms. This added another £12,873 to the bill, and took four leisurely years to complete. It was not until January 1759 that the new institution was actually opened for public inspection.

By that time the new museum had received a new administrative framework. Sloane's original Trustees had been replaced by the forty-one Trustees stipulated by the Act of 1753: six Family Trustees – representatives of the families of Cotton, Harley and Sloane; twenty Official Trustees – holders of specific offices: the Archbishop of Canterbury, the Lord Chancellor and the Speaker of the House of Commons (the three Principal Trustees), the Lord President of the Council, the First Lord of the Treasury (Prime Minister), the Lord Privy Seal, the First Lord of the Admiralty, the two principal Secretaries of State, the Lord Steward, the Lord Chamberlain, the Bishop of London, the Chancellor of the Exchequer, the Lord Chief Justice of England, the Master of the Rolls, the Lord Chief Justice of the Common Pleas, the Attorney-General, the President of the Royal Society and the President of the [Royal] College of Physicians; and fifteen Elected Trustees – that is, elected by the other twenty-six. The Principal Trustees were empowered to appoint all Officers of the Museum, except the Principal Librarian, who was appointed by the Crown on their advice. As private benefactions increased, so did the number of Family Trustees – the Townley, Elgin and Payne Knight families being all eventually represented, as well as a representative of the Crown. To these were later added the Presidents of the Royal Academy of Arts and the Society of Antiquaries. Thus control of the British Museum was from the outset removed from the arena of party politics, and placed in the hands of the chief officers of church and state, private benefactors, and the leaders of the learned professions.

It was certainly a powerful administration. And its structure survived more or less intact until 1963. But could the Trustees be trusted to act in the public interest? For the first half century of its existence the British Museum was scarcely a public institution in the modern sense. It reflected the restricted horizons of its political founders. Like the eighteenth-century House of Commons it seemed to distinguish, implicitly at least, between the People and the Populace. The 1753 Act had stipulated that 'free access . . . be given to all studious and curious Persons'. But as one of the first Trustees put it, in 1759: 'a general liberty to ordinary people of all ranks and denominations, is not to be kept within bounds. Many irregularities will be committed that cannot be prevented by a few librarians who will soon be insulted by such people, if they offer to control or contradict them.' Access to the museum was therefore hedged about by innumerable restrictions. First there were the exceptions to the days of opening: 'except Saturday and Sunday in each week'; 'except Christmas day and one week after'; 'except the week after Easter Sunday and the week after Whit-Sunday'; and 'except Good Friday, and all days which are now, or shall hereafter be specially appointed for Thanksgivings or fasts by public authority'. Then there were the restricted hours of opening: at first the museum was open for only three hours a day, then it was laid down that 'between the months of September and April inclusive, from Monday to Friday inclusive, the museum be opened, from nine o'clock in the morning till three in the afternoon; and likewise at the same hours on Tuesday, Wednesday and Thursday, in May, June, July and August; but on Monday and Friday, only from four o'clock to eight in the afternoon, during those four months, except at the times above stated.' Finally, there was the problem of admission: applicants had first to present themselves at the porter's lodge, then fill in their name, condition and address in the porter's register, then pass the scrutiny of the librarians, then wait until their ticket had been formally issued, before they could enter into the holy of holies. It was a process which took several weeks and two or three visits. Needless to say, no children were admitted. The armed sentries at the entrance – not removed until 1863 – must have reinforced the impression that Britain's Temple of the Arts was indeed a citadel of culture.

Still, it must be remembered that, at the same time, these conditions were more lenient than those of any other major European collection. François de la Rochefoucauld noted with approval in 1784 that the British Museum had been created expressly 'for the instruction and gratification of the public'. During its first twenty years, it attracted an average of 10,000 visitors per annum. And they were all admitted free of charge. Only once did the idea of charging for admission come near to being accepted. In 1774 General Conway suggested to the House of Commons 'that no person be admitted to see the curiosities without paying; [and] that every person who gave extraordinary trouble should pay an extraordinary price'. Happily, the motion was defeated. As regards public opening, the Trustees were pioneers. They were the first to wrestle with that eternal conundrum: security versus accessibility. 'This Museum,' they concluded, 'though chiefly designed for the use of learned and studious men, both natives and foreigners, in their re-searches into the several parts of knowledge; yet being a national establishment, founded by authority of Parliament . . . the advantages accruing from it should be rendered as general as possible; but as it is of a more extensive nature than any other before established, it doth require some particular rules and restrictions . . .'

When eighteenth-century visitors at last entered the British Museum, what did they find? In the first place, of course, they found Montagu House [16]. The first Montagu House had been built in 1675–80 by Ralph Montagu, diplomat and rake, Master of the Great Wardrobe to Charles II, and 1st Duke of Montagu (1638–1709). His political career was long and treacherous, even by Restoration standards. Swift called him 'as arrant a knave as any in his time'. But as a patron of the arts his taste was impeccable. It was he who imported Verrio from France to England in 1672 and secured him a post in the Mortlake tapestry works.

16. The Garden Front, Montagu House,
at the time of the Gordon Riots (1780), Paul Sandby.

Congreve inserted a graceful dedication to Montagu as Maecenas in his preface to *The Way of the World* in 1699. 'If I am not mistaken,' he wrote, 'poetry is the only art which has not yet laid claim to your lordship's patronage. Architecture and painting, to the great honour of our country, have flourished under your influence and protection.' Montagu was in fact a patron who made money like a rogue and spent it like a gentleman. Over many years he dissipated several fortunes – he married two rich and noble widows, one foolish, one mad – while constructing and reconstructing his town and country residences: Montagu House, Bloomsbury; Ditton Park, Buckinghamshire; Boughton, Northamptonshire; and his official lodging in the Cockpit, Whitehall. At Montagu House he employed Robert Hooke (1635-1703), a hunch-backed scientist and architect, colleague of Sir Christopher Wren and Curator of the Royal Society. John Evelyn twice visited the newly completed mansion and found it a '*fine palace*, built after the French pavilion way', with superb frescoes by Verrio and 'some excellent paintings of Holbein and other masters'. As for interior decoration, he thought 'there was nothing more glorious in England'. According to Montagu's cousin William, Verrio's 'Labours of Hercules' made the great room on the first floor unique among painted rooms in England. The house was clearly Hooke's *chef d'oeuvre* and a convincing example of his Gallic tastes – his Bedlam Hospital (1675-6) was said to have been copied from the Tuileries; Louis XIV replied by commissioning an adaptation of St James's for 'offices of the vilest nature'. All in all, Ralph Montagu's Bloomsbury seat must have been London's finest example of that 'Gallomania' which transformed English architecture and interior decoration between the Restoration and the Glorious Revolution.

One night in January 1686 this first Montagu House was gutted by fire. The Duke, as might be expected from a man who was Ambassador to the court of Louis XIV, is said to have imported a Frenchman named Poujet or Poughet to supervise reconstruction. Traditionally, this is assumed to be Pierre Puget (1622-94) of Marseilles, 'the French Michael Angelo'. Now, the style of Puget's best-known work, the Hotel de Ville at Toulon, makes this attribution unlikely. In 1678 Puget was hard at work on his Milo and his relief of Alexander and Diogenes. And there is no record that he ever came to England at all. But the only alternative which has so far come to light – a French interior decorator by the name of Boujet – seems at best equally doubtful. Clearly a French designer was employed, as for Montagu's country seat at Boughton (1687-1705), a house traditionally 'contrived after the manner of Versailles'. According to legend, the French Ambassador used to reside at Montagu House while Montagu was at Versailles, and Louis XIV agreed to share the cost of reconstruction provided French workmen were employed. Anyway, it was this second Montagu House – Hooke's exterior plus the mysterious Frenchman's interior – which became the British Museum.

The plan of Montagu House resembled that of a Parisian hotel, *entre cour et jardin*. A cupola'd entrance, known as Montagu Great Gate –

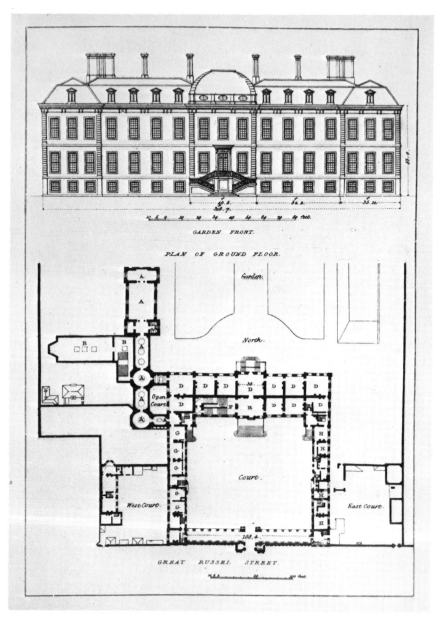

GARDEN FRONT.

PLAN OF GROUND FLOOR.

17. The Old British Museum, Montagu House, garden front and ground plan

18. Front quadrangle of Montagu House (*c.* 1842), John Wykeham Archer

strikingly reminiscent of Hooke's Royal College of Surgeons (1672–8) –
gave access to a quadrangular court with a colonnade of Ionic columns
linked to the main block by extensive outbuildings [18]. The house
was built of brick, with stone quoins. Its ponderous, square-domed roof
and dormer windows certainly gave it a French flavour. The central *corps
de logis* clearly echoes Lemercier's Château de Richelieu (begun 1631), as
well as the contemporary garden fronts of Clagny and Choisy-le-Roi.

Inside, the parquetry floors and painted ceilings produced an indubit-
ably Gallic impression. The interior frescoes were in fact all the work of
imported French artists, mostly Huguenots: Jacques Rousseau, much
employed at Marly; Charles de Lafosse, a pupil of Le Brun, whose
greatest work was the dome of the Invalides; Jean Baptiste Monnoyer,
who also worked at Boughton; and Jacques Parmentier, who seems to
have been mostly employed as an assistant. We know that Lafosse was

19. The Entrance Hall of Montagu House (c. 1845), George Scharf Sr

responsible for the figure subjects, Parmentier for the feigned sculpture, and Rousseau for the landscape background and architectural framing. Monnoyer presumably contributed some of his inimitable flower-paintings. These decorations progressed slowly during the 1690s. We also know the names of the principal English craftsmen: Henry Dogood, plasterer; John Dandridge, painter; and Roger Davis, joiner. All three came from the orbit of the Office of Works, and were also employed at Boughton. During the first decade of the eighteenth century further painted decorations were added by Louis Chéron, John Dandridge and Sir James Thornhill. The total effect must have been one of immense richness. Several fine items were later transferred to Boughton, including a notable series of sketches by Van Dyck. But most of the work at Montagu House can now only be enjoyed vicariously, in George Scharf's eloquent watercolours [19, 20], executed in the 1840s, just before the old British Museum was demolished. Only one interior fragment survives in Bloomsbury: the massive altarpiece from Ralph Montagu's chapel, now in Hawksmoor's St George's church.

As the eighteenth century wore on, the style of Montagu House seemed first grand, then unfashionable, and finally curious – almost comic. E. Hutton's *New View of London* (1708) takes the building seriously, and describes it as 'an extraordinary, noble and beautiful palace . . . The inside . . . richly furnished and beautifully finished; [with a] . . . great variety of noble paintings of the Ionic Order.' But by 1736 taste had changed. The *New Critical Review of Public Buildings of London* complains that 'Montagu House has been long, though ridiculously, esteemed as one of the most beautiful buildings about the town . . . the entrance into the court-yard is mean and Gothic [i.e. debased], more like the portal of a monastery than the gate of a palace . . . and the body of the house has no other recommendation than merely its bulk and the quantity of space that it fills.'

By the middle of the eighteenth century this judgement seemed irreversible. The best that Horace Walpole could say was that 'what it wants in grace and beauty, is compensated by the spaciousness and lofty magnificence of the apartments'. But by 1814 Montagu House was sufficiently antique to be treated as a piece of architectural history. In that year the *Gentleman's Magazine* printed a detailed survey of the fabric by the antiquary John Carter, comparing its design to the Château de Breves, the Château de Coulommiers by Saloman de Brosse, the Tuileries, Lemercier's Château de Richelieu, Perrault's Château de Sceaux, and even to Versailles. All these examples seemed to share the chief characteristics of the British Museum:

external dead-walls or façades, lodges, with carriage entrance, large court or courts, colonnades, offices in wings, grand mass in line for state apartments, in a centre, with continuous, and projecting masses at each extremity . . . Large and rich doorways and windows, rustic quoins (no vertical joints), deep entablatures, extreme lofty roofs in pyramidal, convex, or concave and dome-wise sweeps, containing one or more storeys of dormer windows, chimneys in breaks etc.

Carter described the frescoed allegories of the interior in detail, including Apollo borrowing Phaeton's chariot on the Grand Stairs, and in the Grand Saloon Nell Gwynne (Minerva) presiding over the fall of Cromwell (Rebellion). Other decorative fittings were compared to designs published by Antoine Le Pautre and Pierre Charmeton during the reign of Louis XIV. 'The whole assemblage of buildings', Carter concluded, 'retain . . . nearly all their first details . . . unadulterated.'

But that was the voice of an antiquary. By the Regency period Montagu House seemed to most people an aesthetic joke and a financial incubus: repairs and alterations cost nearly £20,000 between 1810 and 1820. When the time came for it to give way to a new British Museum, Charles Lamb was almost alone in shedding tears for 'the princely apartments of poor condemned Montagu House'.

20. The Great Staircase, Montagu House (c. 1845), George Scharf Sr

Meanwhile, how well did Montagu House function as a British Museum? The keynote of the collection was struck in the entrance hall [19]. Here the curious visitor began to thread his way between oriental idols, marble busts, elephants and sponges; polar bears, portraits, fossils and meteorites; Roubiliac's statue of Shakespeare, Chantrey's statue of Banks, and several stuffed giraffes. Then up the great staircase [20], with its broad and easy treads ('for the thigh is exercised more in elevation than in distension'), and into the saloon pausing perhaps to gaze at the painted nymphs and deities on the way – restored by Rigaud in the Regency period. When Celia Fiennes came here she found the *trompe l'oeil* so convincing that she could hardly find the right way out. These major rooms made no pretence at being anything more than a miscellany. But in the remainder of the museum there was some attempt at sub-division. There were originally three departments: Manuscripts, Medals and Coins in six rooms on the east side of the principal floor; Natural and Artificial Productions in the corresponding rooms on the west side; and Printed Books, Maps, Globes and Drawings in all twelve rooms on the ground floor. The titles were certainly sweeping. In particular, 'Natural and Artificial Productions' turned out to be the ancestor of no less than eleven modern departments: six at Bloomsbury (Egyptian Antiquities, Western Asiatic Antiquities, Greek and Roman Antiquities, British and Medieval Antiquities, Oriental Antiquities and Ethnography), and five at Kensington (Zoology, Entomology, Mineralogy, Botany and Palaeontology). No wonder Saint Fond's reaction in 1786 was highly critical. 'The British Museum', he noted in his *Travels* (1799), 'contains many collections . . . but, with the exception of some fishes in a small apartment, which are begun to be classed, nothing is in order, everything is out of its place; and this assemblage appears rather an immense magazine, in which things have been thrown at random, than a scientific collection, destined to instruct and honour a great nation.' More simply, Cobbett christened Montagu House 'the old curiosity shop'.

But eighteenth-century Bloomsbury was not the only place where techniques of classification were still in their infancy. Museums still consisted

> '. . . Of unicorns and alligators,
> Elks, mermaids, mummies, witches, satyrs,
> And twenty other stranger matters.'

Labels were actually in use in the Plater Museum at Basle in 1663 and in the Aldrovandi Museum at Bologna in 1688. Yet this was not a practice which was widely copied. The antique classifications of Samuel van Quicheberg's *Inscriptiones* (1565) continued to confuse rather than elucidate collections throughout Europe for more than two centuries. This was the so-called 'universal' system followed by Tradescant and Ashmole. Not until the 1820s was the Ashmolean Museum rearranged by John Shute Duncan and his brother Philip Bury Duncan. And even then they managed to set out natural history specimens according to the plan of Dr Paley's *Natural Theology*, 'to induce a mental habit of associating the view of natural phenomena with the conviction that they are the media of Divine manifestation'. The display of paintings and antiquities was slightly more advanced. C. F. Neickelius had produced in 1727 his famous *Museographica*, the first handbook of museology; and in the years after 1781 Christian von Mechel had rearranged the galleries at Vienna along chronological lines. But during its first half century the British Museum was strongest not in fine art and antiquities, but in books, manuscripts and natural history specimens. And in the classification and display of natural history exhibits there were no satisfactory precedents until the opening of William Stark's new Hunterian Museum at Glasgow (1804) [31] and George Dance's Hunterian Gallery in the Royal College of Surgeons, Lincoln's Inn Fields (1806–13).

Still, the early arrangements at the British Museum seem to have been unnecessarily chaotic. In 1765 a French visitor, P. J. Grosley, thought the museum grand but the service poor. Montagu House he considered 'the largest, the most stately, the best arranged, and most richly decorated' structure of its kind in England. But the Printed Book section seemed weak by comparison with the Natural History collections. And he gave only limited praise to the civility of the curators. 'They shew', he remarked, 'the most obliging readiness to explain things to the visitor, but their very courtesy is wont to make a stranger content himself with hasty and unsatisfactory glances, that he may not trespass on their politeness.' By 1776 visitors applying for admission in April were still waiting for their tickets in August. Yet most foreigners, after gaining access, came away agreeably impressed. F. A. Wendeborn's *View of England* (translated from the German, 1791) notes that individual sections might be paralleled elsewhere. But he urges visitors to inspect 'these large and lofty rooms, dedicated to the Muses', 'for the whole is costly, worth seeing, and honourable to the Nation; [and] when taken together it has not its equal'.

Spurred on by Wendeborn, Karl Philip Moritz of Berlin arrived in 1782 and left us a nice description of the old British Museum:

In general, you must give in your name a fortnight before you can be admitted. But by the kindness of Mr Woide [a German Assistant Librarian], I got admission earlier . . . Yet after all, I am sorry to say that it was the room, the glass-cases, the shelves . . . which I saw; not the museum itself, so rapidly were we hurried on through the departments. The company who saw it when I did, and in like manner, was variously composed. They were of all sorts, and some, as I believe, of the very lowest classes of people of both sexes, for, as it is the property of the Nation, every one has the same 'right' – I use the term of the country – to see it that another has. I had Mr Wendeborn's books in my pocket, and it, at least, enabled me to take more particular notice of some of the principal things . . . The Gentleman who conducted us took little pains to conceal the contempt which he felt for my communications when he found it was only a German description . . . which I had . . . So rapid a passage through a vast suite of rooms in little more than one hour of time, with opportunity to cast but one poor longing look of astonishment on all the vast treasures of nature, antiquity and literature, in the examination of which one might profitably spend years, confuses, stuns and overpowers the visitor.

Two years later an Englishman, William Hutton of Birmingham, was less polite. After buying admission from a ticket tout for two shillings, he was rushed through the museum in thirty minutes flat. He probably spent longer composing this classic description in his *Journey to London* (1785):

I was not likely to forget Tuesday, December 7th, at eleven . . . We began to move pretty fast, when I asked with some surprise whether there were none to inform us what the curiosities were as we went on? A tall genteel young man *in person*, who seemed to be our conductor, replied with some warmth: 'What! would you have me tell you everything in the Museum? How is it possible? Besides, are not the names written upon many of them?' I was much too humbled by this reply to utter another word. The company seemed influenced; they made haste and were silent. No voice was heard but in whispers. If a man spends two minutes in a room, in which a thousand things demand his attention, he cannot bestow on them a glance apiece. When our leader opens the door of another apartment, the silent language of that action is, *come along* . . . I considered myself in the midst of a rich entertainment, consisting of ten thousand rarities, but, like Tantalus, I could not taste one. It grieved me to think how much I lost for want of a little information. In about thirty minutes we finished our silent journey through the princely mansion, which could well have taken thirty days. I went out much about as wise as I went in, but with this severe reflection that, for fear of losing my chance, I had that morning abruptly torn myself from three gentlemen with whom I was engaged in an interesting conversation, had lost my breakfast, got wet to the skin, spent half-a-crown in coach-hire, paid two shillings for a ticket, [and] been hackneyed through the rooms with violence . . . I had laid more stress on the British Museum, than on anything else which I should see in London. It was the only sight which disgusted me . . . Government purchased this rare collection . . . at a vast expense, and exhibits it as a national honour. . . . How far it answers the end proposed this chapter of cross incidents will testify.

Such criticisms were only slowly answered. Not until 1805 were admission tickets abolished. Not until 1808 was an official Synopsis of the museum's contents at last produced. And only in 1810 were 'strangers' free to roam the galleries at will. Even then the Trustees maintained that their chief aim was to further 'Science and the Arts', not to gratify 'the curiosity of . . . multitudes . . . in quest of amusement'. In the museum's early days no more than sixty visitors a day had been the rule. In 1808 it was customary to admit one hundred and twenty in groups of fifteen on any of the first four days of the week, Friday being reserved for artists. But by 1810 the museum was open on Monday, Wednesday and Friday from ten to four, and 'any person of decent appearance' who applied 'between the hours of ten and two' was at last admitted without a ticket and even allowed to 'tarry in the apartments or the Gallery of Antiquities without any limitation of time, except the shutting of the house at four o'clock'. Three days a week remained the rule for many years. Daily opening was only instituted in 1879. And as late as 1836 the Principal Librarian, Sir Henry Ellis, openly defended the closing of the museum on Saturdays, Sundays and public holidays: it was his job to keep out 'the more vulgar class', such as 'sailors from the dock yards and girls whom they might bring with them'. The opening up of Britain's museum was certainly a slow process.

It was, of course, really a question of finance. Having founded the British Museum, Parliament nearly let it founder by starving the establishment of regular funds. It was precisely because the staff were so few in number and so poorly paid that accessibility was so limited – there were insufficient warders to place one in each room. Parliamentary grants for specific purchases were available only on an *ad hoc* basis. The museum's annual income from endowments was meagre. In its first half century the British Museum could hardly have expanded its collections at all had it not been for private benefactions: the sums expended by the Trustees in purchases during the early decades seldom totalled £100 per annum. And it was in fact these benefactions, private and royal – supplemented on several crucial occasions by specific Parliamentary grants – which eventually transformed the character and appearance of the old British Museum as it struggled out of the eighteenth and into the nineteenth century.

First came the Thomason Tracts, an incomparable series of seventeenth-century pamphlets presented by George III in 1762. Then came a set of Parliamentary papers in 1772. In the same year the antique vases of Sir William Hamilton arrived, purchased by Parliament for £8,400. In 1799 came an exquisite library built up by a solitary bibliophile, Clayton Mordaunt Cracherode. And in 1802 the Egyptian antiquities, captured when the French surrendered Alexandria, arrived – and so, by conquest, the Rosetta Stone became the property of the British public. Three years later came the Townley Marbles. These Greek and Roman antiquities, collected by Charles Townley, scion of an old Catholic family from Lancashire, had for some years been exhibited to *cognoscenti* in a private gallery in Mayfair. They were now bought by Parliament in two instalments in 1804 and 1814 for £28,200. In 1807 the Lansdowne Manuscripts arrived, a worthy supplement to the Cottonian collection, accumulated by the 1st Marquess of Lansdowne and secured by Parliament for some £5,000. In 1810 Parliament purchased the mineral collection of Charles Greville for £13,727. And these were only the most striking acquisitions of the British Museum's first half century.

Among these many acquisitions, three – the Hamilton, Townley and Egyptian collections – filled an obvious gap in the museum's coverage. In 1807 a fourth department, of Antiquities, was therefore established to deal with them, and a new wing was constructed to house them as Montagu House was already overcrowded. This new Townley Gallery [21–5], begun in 1804 and opened by royal visit on 3 June 1808, marked the first stage in the extension and reconstruction of Montagu House. It

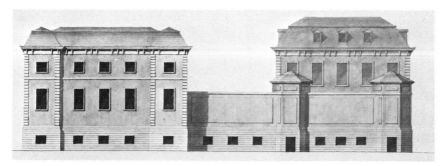

21. Design for the Townley Gallery in the style of Montagu House (1803), G. Saunders

was designed by the Trustees' architect George Saunders (*c.* 1762–1839), a man of competence rather than talent, and reproduced in its scale and arrangement the atmosphere of a private sculpture gallery: Townley's bust by Nollekens was appropriately placed over the entrance. In fact Townley told the principal Librarian, Sir Joseph Planta, that the new buildings should be 'a pattern to be followed in this improved age . . . without pretensions to expensive magnificence or fantastic novelty'. The new wing originally contained thirteen small rooms arranged in sequence in the form of a right-angled extension to the main building: one room each for terra-cottas, Roman and sepulchral antiquities, Roman antiquities and coins and medals; five for Greek and Roman sculptures; two for Egyptian antiquities; one for the Hamilton vase collection; and one for drawings and engravings. These new galleries were linked to Montagu House by two passages, top-lit by circular tribunes, and cost in all £28,000.

But scarcely had this expansion been consolidated when a new wave of acquisitions forced the Trustees to think again. Five collections of international importance arrived within little more than a decade. In 1814–15 the Elgin Marbles were bought by Parliament for £35,000. In 1815–16 the Phigaleian Marbles, discovered by the architect C. R. Cockerell, were bought for £19,000. Soon afterwards, in 1824, came the

22. Design for the Townley Gallery (1803), G. Saunders

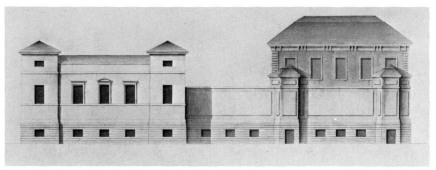

23. Design for the Townley Gallery, cross section (1803), G. Saunders

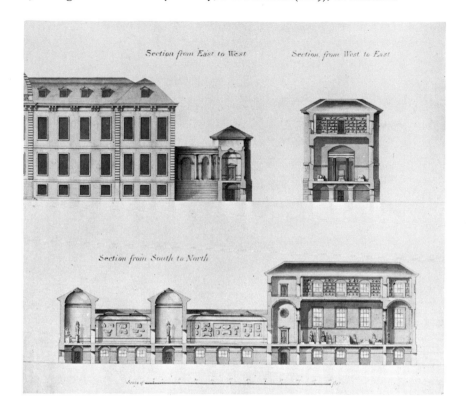

books, bronzes and drawings bequeathed by that 'priapic' pundit of the Picturesque, Richard Payne Knight (1750–1824). Three years later Sir Joseph Banks bequeathed his celebrated library, his ethnographical collections and his botanical specimens. And, last but not least, the early 1820s also saw the arrival of the royal library built up by George III and 'given' to the museum by George IV in return for a secret payment of £180,000 from the droits of the Admiralty.

The arrival of the Hamilton, Alexandrian, Townley, Elgin, Phigaleian and Payne Knight collections transformed the old British Museum.

24. The Townley Gallery, interior, G. Saunders

Within a generation, almost accidentally, Montagu House had become one of the world's leading depositories of antique sculpture. Archaeology had replaced natural history as the backbone of the museum's collections. Knight's bequest alone was valued at £60,000. His Greek coins put London ahead of Paris; his bronzes outdistanced the famous collection at Naples. But it was, of course, the Elgin Marbles which confirmed the museum's international reputation in the field of classical antiquities. Yet when they were first unpacked at Bloomsbury they had to be put in a prefabricated shed. More and more, in both style and scale, Montagu House seemed ludicrously inadequate as the home of a British Museum. In 1826 Prince Pückler-Muskau called it 'a strange "Mismach" of works of art, natural curiosities, books and models, preserved in a miserable building'. But by that date a scheme for a new British Museum had already been born. And this time there were to be no half measures, no architectural compromises. The new British Museum was to be a veritable Temple of the Arts, recalling in its very structure the glories of ancient Greece.

25. The Townley Gallery: arrangement of exhibits

26. *Sir Robert Smirke*, 1828. Bust by E. H. Baily

3 : Sir Robert Smirke and the Greek Revival

'The Greeks were gods' (Henry Fuseli, 1807)

The architect chosen to design Britain's Temple of the Muses was a diminutive, middle-aged man named Robert Smirke [26]. Who was he? How did he come to design the British Museum? And what is his status in British architectural history?

Born in 1780, Smirke was the son of a minor Royal Academician, Robert Smirke Sr (1751–1845). As a satirist in painting and prose, the elder Smirke was not untalented. 'His designs', remarked Southey, 'will sell any book, be it ever so bad.' And he is still remembered as the illustrator of *Don Quixote* and Boydell's *Shakespeare*. But it was his talents as an intriguer – he was known as the abbé Seyes of the Royal Academy – which in the long run had the greatest impact on his son's career. Even among Academicians – that 'nest of vermin' as Northcote called them – the elder Smirke was reckoned a hard fighter, a 'man of strong likings and dislikings'. But his ambitions were for his family rather than himself. And in this respect he was very successful. He had twelve children. Three died young. One son entered the navy, two more the civil service. One daughter, Mary, made a name as an artist; another, Sarah, married into a great contracting family, the Bakers of Rochester; one son, Richard, would probably have become a well-known topographical painter, had he not died in his thirties; another son, the future Sir Edward Smirke (1795–1875) became a well-known legal antiquary and Attorney General to the Prince of Wales; and two more sons followed their father into the Royal Academy – Sir Robert Smirke (1780–1867), architect of the new British Museum, and Sydney Smirke (1798–1877), architect of the museum's Round Reading Room.

Young Robert Smirke was quickly marked out for an architectural career. At fifteen, as Head Boy at Aspley School near Woburn, he read Latin, Greek and French, and showed 'an inclination towards drawing'. In March 1796, on the recommendation of George Dance, he was admitted free of charge into the office of the future Sir John Soane. Ten months later he withdrew, hurt by Soane's peevish manner, and instead became Dance's private pupil. Soane never forgot the implied insult. But the move did Smirke's career no harm at all. Away from the 'poor, dear old tyrant' of Lincoln's Inn Fields, his talents rapidly improved. In 1796 he won the Royal Academy Silver Medal and the Silver Palette of the Society of Arts, Manufactures and Commerce. And – prophetically enough – in 1799 he won the Royal Academy Gold Medal with a *Design for a National Museum*. Then away he went for four years – between 1801 and 1805 – on an extended Grand Tour. It was, of course, war time and his adventures make startling reading. Disguised as an American in Paris, beset by bandits in Greece, locked up in a lazaretto at Messina, dancing at a masked ball in Rome, waltzing in Vienna, travelling across the Morea on foot, by mule or on horseback, sleeping in cow-sheds, living off roast sheep and retsina, bribing Turkish officials for fragments of the Acropolis, taking measurements in the burning sun, making drawings under armed guard – no wonder his parents kept every one of his letters. Fortunate, too, that their son wrote so carefully: historians can trace step by step this rigorous architectural apprenticeship. Through his enthusiastic eyes – in Brussels, Paris, Berlin, Potsdam, Prague, Dresden, Vienna, Florence, Venice, Padua, Genoa, Vicenza, Rome, Naples, Corinth, Athens, Delphi, Thebes, Olympia – we can watch the emergence of a Neo-classicist, the making of a Greek Revivalist. No wonder Joseph Farington, 'the Dictator of the Academy', thought young Smirke 'the best educated artist in his line that this country has produced'.

Smirke's professional progress was extraordinarily swift. The Napoleonic Wars hardly made it easy to build up a large architectural practice:

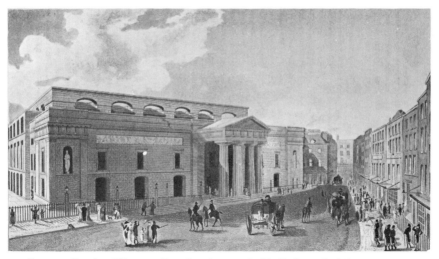

27. Covent Garden Theatre, London (1808–9), Sir Robert Smirke

he was himself a keen militia man. But within two years of his return to England his private practice had been established. Within four years he was famous as the designer of a revolutionary London theatre [27]. Within ten years he had reached the top of his profession as one of the three architects officially attached to the Office of Works. Influence made him Architect to the Royal Mint in 1807. An expanding reputation made him Surveyor to the Inner Temple (1819) and the Duchy of Lancaster (1820). And in the 1830s he united the functions of architect, surveyor and town planner by replanning the approaches to London Bridge. As early as 1808 Farington observed: 'he now pays *clerks* who assist him to the amount of £700 per annum'. By 1815 the sculptor Rossi was complaining that the new 'Smirkish' fashion for simplicity in interior decoration – so different to the 'embroidery snippets' of the Adam-Wyatt school – had reduced the cost of chimneypieces from £50 or £60 to less than a quarter of that sum. And with popularity went prestige. In 1805 he joined both the Architect's Club and the Society of Antiquaries. In

1808 he was elected A.R.A.; in 1811, R.A., and from 1820 onwards he acted as the Royal Academy's Treasurer.

Soon Smirke had more work than he could manage. In 1809 Farington noted that 'Lord Lansdowne and others have offered commissions to him which he cannot now accept'. Three years later, at a time of national crisis, he was working simultaneously on Lowther and Eastnor Castles, the Mint, the bridges at Carlisle and Gloucester, and the Court Houses at Carlisle – all major commissions which together cost over £500,000. With the easing of building restrictions after 1815, Smirke's provincial commitments increased rapidly: the Wellington Testimonial at Dublin, Court Houses at Gloucester and Hereford and a dozen country house commissions. Weeks were spent in coach travelling. In October 1814 he was in Rochester, in November he embarked on 'a month's excursion to the North, Gloucester and Hereford, to inspect the progress of works carrying on'. In September 1815 he visited 'the North of England, and the neighbourhood of Kelso, an excursion of three weeks', returning via Lowther and Cambridge. In June 1816 he returned from Scotland after a month's absence, having covered eleven hundred miles. After obtaining the commission to design the County Buildings at Perth in 1814, his Scottish practice flourished. In 1818 Farington noted: 'Smirke spoke of his excursions to Scotland and of the time they took as being inconvenient. Every time he goes he refuses offers of commissions, but he has now many works in hand in that country: viz. for the Marquis of Queensbury, Lord Wemyss, Mr Balfour, Mr James Drummond . . . and others.' No wonder it was noticed in 1815 that the industrious architect looked 'ill, worn and out of condition'.

Eighteen fifteen was also the year of Smirke's elevation to the Office of Works. It was by virtue of his position as Attached Architect that he came to design the British Museum. And the story of that appointment makes a nice example of Regency intrigue.

Between 1718, when Wren was dismissed by the Whigs, and 1782, when Burke purged the department of sinecurists, the position of Surveyor General had been a political appointment. Between 1782 and 1796 the Surveyor Generalship had been held by Sir William Chambers, a conscientious administrator and a most professional architect. His successor was James Wyatt, a man of very different stamp. As an architect Wyatt's undisciplined talent occasionally came near to genius. As an administrator he was a disaster, hovering on the border between negligence and corruption. Inevitably, in 1812, a government inquiry was set in motion. But one September Saturday in 1813, before the investigators had time to recommend the Surveyor General's dismissal, James Wyatt – 'the Destroyer' – was killed in a coach accident. His enemies were delighted: Benjamin West confessed himself 'much struck . . . he said it would be upon his mind for forty eight hours'. And his rivals rejoiced: Nash, Soane, Smirke and Porden all showed themselves hungry for office, to say nothing of Wyatt's son Philip, and his nephews Benjamin and Jeffry. Soane trusted to his contacts in Whitehall, notably the Prime Minister Lord Liverpool. Nash relied on his royal friends at Windsor and St James's – after all, he had worked at Carlton House and Windsor Castle. Porden hoped at least for preferment in the Ordnance Office, one of Wyatt's lesser sinecures. Jeffry Wyatt wrote no less than fifteen letters to different people 'soliciting their interest to get something that his uncle enjoyed'. With his patron the Duke of Wellington abroad, Benjamin Wyatt fell back on the influence of the Duke of Richmond. Philip Wyatt adopted shock tactics. Bursting into the royal bedchamber at 3 o'clock in the morning, he delivered himself of the 'melancholy account' which 'very much affected the Regent even to shedding tears'. But when he proceeded with the 'real business', namely 'to solicit the Regent to bestow upon him such of the advantages possessed by his late father as His Royal Highness might think proper', the Regent merely 'returned a civil answer in a general way'. By comparison, Smirke was much more diplomatic. He received news of the accident in a hasty note from his father, and immediately took a chaise from Hastings to London in time to send letters by the evening post. These letters marshalled his supporters: the ruling côterie of Royal Academicians and a battery of influential Tories. And these supporters in turn wrote letters to friends in strategic positions in court or government. For a few months the Royal Academy buzzed with jobs and rumours of jobs. West remarked that 'he pitied those who had obligations upon them to leave London at this season so favourable for professional application.' In the the end, after Nash had temporarily acted as Wyatt's successor during 1814, the Board of the Office of Works was reorganized and all three leading candidates – Nash, Soane and Smirke – were given the post of Attached Architect under the direction of a non-professional Surveyor General.

For Smirke the great intrigue was a tremendous triumph. Nash and Soane were both elderly men at the top of their profession. He was only thirty-five. And one of his new colleagues was his former tutor. Royal and government buildings were divided between the three men on a roughly geographical basis. One M.P. called 'their respective governments . . . as absolute as that of any Roman praetor in his province'. And although the commission for Buckingham Palace went to Nash, and the new government offices and law courts went to Soane, Smirke was hardly short of work. Apart from routine administration, which he did very well, he was responsible for several new buildings, including an extension to Somerset House (with which may be linked a private commission, the erection of King's College); the completion of the Royal Mint and London Custom House; and the construction of the British Museum and General Post Office. Perhaps the glamorous jobs went to Nash and Soane, but the most profitable ones went to Smirke. 'Our appointments', Nash told Soane, 'are perfectly Constitutional, I the King, you the Lords, and *your* friend Smirke, the Commons . . .'

After this appointment Smirke became more and more a London architect. His connection with the Office of Works, as well as his work at Millbank Penitentiary, the Inner Temple, and several clubs and private mansions, drew him inevitably to the capital. His London Bridge

Approaches led eventually to his appointment to the Commission for Metropolitan Improvements. As an assessor and referee, he was always in great demand. And with the retirement of Nash and Soane, Smirke became the doyen of metropolitan architects, until his eclipse by Sir Charles Barry. In fact, more than any other architect except Wren and Nash, he moulded the metropolis in his own image. In the General Post Office and the British Museum alone, he was handling – during the 1820s – commissions worth upwards of £1,000,000. The cost of his street improvements around London Bridge later made even that figure seem small. It was actually rumoured that he used to turn down jobs worth less than £10,000. When he died in 1867, after more than twenty years' retirement, he was still worth £90,000. His total list of works certainly makes impressive reading: apart from a score of unexecuted designs, he worked on more than twenty churches, more than fifty public buildings and more than sixty private houses. In sheer bulk, his practice more than matches up to those of Nash, Soane or any of the Wyatts. He even rivalled Sir Charles Barry. No wonder the chorus, in Planché's burlesque of Aristophanes' *Birds* (1846), chanted:

> Go to work – rival Smirke –
> Make a dash, à la Nash –
> Something try at, worthy Wyatt –
> Plans out carry, great as Barry.

The explanation of Smirke's astonishing success can be summed up in one word: patronage. Smirke was a Tory architect. He wore a political label in much the same way as James Gibbs or Henry Holland. He had no need of that Victorian fetish, the architectural competition. His early patrons were almost exclusively Tory at a time when the Whigs were in the political wilderness. Inherited friends in the Royal Academy, such as Benjamin West, Sir Thomas Lawrence, George Dance and Joseph Farington, introduced him to an army of influential patrons – men like the eccentric Lord Abercorn, the amiable Lord Oxford, and Pitt's

28. The Old Council House, Bristol (1824-7), Sir Robert Smirke

closest colleague, Henry Dundas, Viscount Melville, 'that Caledonian Hercules'. Then there was John Wilson Croker, editor of the *Quarterly Review*, founder of the Athenaeum and inventor of the word 'Conservative'; Sir George Beaumont, that 'giant of amateurs'; 'Athenian' Aberdeen, and the notorious Marquis of Hertford; pig-tailed Tories like Earl Bathurst and 'Mad Jack' Fuller; romantic Tories like Sir Walter Scott and Sir Alexander Don; as well as celebrities like John Philip Kemble and scholars like Samuel Lysons, the antiquary. Perhaps the *Polytechnic Magazine* had Smirke in mind when it remarked in 1841: 'Artists may live in nearly total seclusion from the world, and their private histories be accordingly very dull, commonplace, and uninteresting; but not so an architect of any eminence, since the very nature of his profession brings him into contact with public men, or with the opulent and the great.' Supremely competent and almost embarrassingly well-connected, Smirke was certainly the Establishment architect *par excellence*.

At least twenty of Smirke's patrons were founder members of the Carlton Club, built to his own designs in 1833-6. Four of his clientèle, Viscount Strathallan, the Earls of Guilford and Powis, and that rabid Tory, the Duke of Newcastle, were numbered among the twenty-two 'stalwarts' who voted in the House of Lords against the third and final reading of the Great Reform Bill, when even the Duke of Wellington had thrown in his hand. But the greatest Tory of them all was William Lowther, Earl of Lonsdale, a genial Maecenas, an early friend of Pitt, a member of the Regent's inner circle, and a patron of Wordsworth, Rogers, Davy and Southey. Lonsdale gave Smirke his first great country house commission, Lowther Castle. Kemble gave him his first public building, Covent Garden Theatre [27]. Bathurst made him architect of the Mint. And Lawrence provided perhaps the greatest prize of all, the friendship of the man who linked Regency with Victorian England, Sir Robert Peel.

According to T. L. Donaldson, Smirke could please 'men whom it was proverbially impossible to please'. Certainly Lonsdale found him 'ingenious, modest and gentlemanly in his manners'. The extent of his patrons' confidence can be measured in two types of public building which Smirke made very much his own: the London club house and the provincial court. Apart from his castellated scheme for Carlisle (1810–12) and his Ionic design at Gloucester (1814–16), all Smirke's county courts are very similar in plan. Dignified and economical, his work at Hereford (1815–17) and Perth (1816–19) is gravely Doric, at Shrewsbury (1836–7) perfunctorily Italianate, at Lincoln (1823–30) cheaply Gothic, and at Maidstone (1824–8) plainly Classical. But at Bristol (1824–7) he came near to achieving the kind of Cockerellian richness which Sir Albert Richardson used to call 'neo-Grec' [28]. As for the London clubs, neither Barry, Nash nor Decimus Burton deserves to be remembered as the architect of London's clubland so much as Sir Robert Smirke, and his younger brother Sydney. The astylar reticence and functional planning of Robert's United Services Club (1817) started a fashion that was copied elsewhere, and which he elaborated with equal success in 1822, at the Union Club and Physicians' College, Trafalgar Square (now Canada House) [29], the Carlton Club, and the Oxford and Cambridge Club (1836–7). Sydney Smirke's design for the Reform Club was rejected, but he assisted his elder brother with the Oxford and Cambridge, rebuilt the Carlton in two sections, and designed the Conservative Club in conjunction with Disraeli's kinsman, George Basevi. Nowhere did the Smirkes' long-standing Tory connections prove more fruitful than in this new sphere of urban architecture.

An analysis of Smirke's professional practice is crucial to any understanding of the workings of Regency patronage. And this is the first reason why he is worth studying. But there is more to him than that. His success can only partly be attributed to the strength of his political connections. When he retired from professional practice in 1844, three of his pupils, C. R. Cockerell, William Burn and Henry Roberts, presented him with a bust by the sculptor Campbell out of 'deep gratitude for important lessons'. The lessons they had in mind amounted to more than

29. The Royal College of Physicians (now part of Canada House), London (1822–5), Sir Robert Smirke

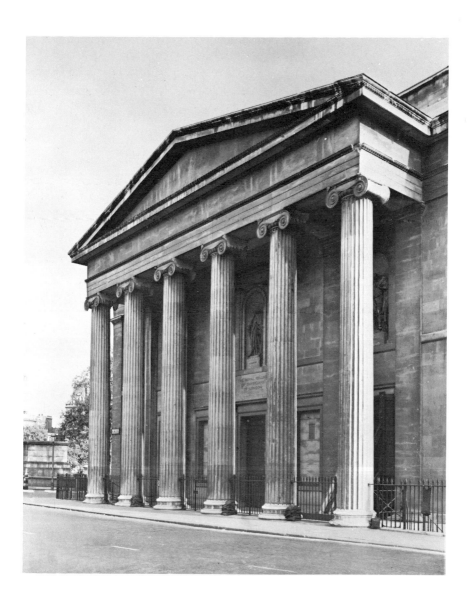

the subtle art of accumulating commissions. Smirke is worth consideration in his own right, as a professional man, as an engineer, and as a
stylist.

As a professional architect-cum-engineer Smirke set up a record
number of 'firsts'. He was the first architect to rationalize the various
eighteenth-century systems of estimating, measuring and cost account-
ing; and the first to employ regularly a new type of assistant, the quantity
surveyor. He became an arbiter on all matters of professional conduct.
He was also a pioneer of modern structural techniques. He was called in
so often to rescue buildings in a state of *rigor mortis* that he came to be
known as 'the Dr Baillie of architects'. At Millbank Penitentiary in 1817,
he was the first to employ concrete foundations, mixed in measured
quantities, and used for load-bearing purposes. The idea was partly John
Rennie's; and in any case lime concrete had already been used independently in France. But to Smirke must go the credit for being the first
British architect to demonstrate the effectiveness of the new technique
on a large scale. And he repeated his performance with still greater éclat
at the London Custom House in 1825. He was probably also the first to
use load-bearing cast iron beams in British domestic architecture. At
Cirencester Park in 1810, he reconstructed the garden front, using 30 foot
cast-iron girders built into the fabric, instead of the customary oak beams.
'Mr Smirke', announced the *Athenaeum* in 1828, 'is pre-eminent in construction: in this respect he has not his superior in the United Kingdom.'

But when Smirke's pupils remembered his 'important lessons' they
were also recalling his contributions as a stylist. His Picturesque castles,
notably Lowther (1806-11), Eastnor (1812-15), and Kinfauns (1820-22)
have considerable pictorial impact. But they are really little more than a
series of scenic devices. Smirke gave the game away when he designed
Lowther with two separate façades, one monastic, the other baronial.
This emphasis on compositional values makes questions of authenticity
or accuracy largely irrelevant. Indeed, the essence of Lowther's 'majestic
pile . . . the stately walls, the pinnacles, the broad embattled brow',

admired by Wordsworth and Southey, lay in the striking manipulation of architectural masses, the superb scenic qualities that now make it peculiarly suitable as a derelict folly. But in relation to the development of the castellated style, Smirke had little to add to the half-statements of Busby's Gwrych (1814) or Wyatt's Ashridge (1808–17). The future there lay with Anthony Salvin. And his tentative essays in Tudoresque or Jacobethan, such as Wilton Castle (*c.* 1810) or Drayton Manor (1831–5), were soon to be eclipsed by Sir Jeffry Wyatville and Sir Charles Barry. Smirke's Gothic detailing often lacks conviction. What Charles Lamb called his 'Gothicisings and Smirkefyings' at the Inner Temple (1816 onwards) were poor examples of a poor period: Picturesque Gothic without the justification of a Picturesque setting. The fact that his scheme for rebuilding the Houses of Parliament (1834–5) was never executed can hardly be regarded as a loss to London. Even his Gothic restorations, notably at York Minster (1830–32), were scarcely more accomplished than James Wyatt's work, merely more cautious.

Smirke's medievalizing was therefore seldom more than a profitable blind alley. His Grecian designs, on the other hand, form an integral part of the Neo-classical revolution.

Neo-classicism in architecture was one of many symptoms associated with the emergence of Romantic art. Of course romanticism is a recurrent impulse – almost an aesthetic neurosis – alternating endlessly with the order and restraint of classical tradition in a kind of creative antiphony. But Romantic is, by convention, a label more usefully and specifically applied to the literature, art and architecture of the late eighteenth and early nineteenth centuries. And under the influence of Romanticism architecture in Europe developed two parallel styles: the Neo Gothic and the Neo Classic. Their application, distribution and rate of progress were very different. But their historicist and functional premises are closely related. The Romantic origins of the Gothic Revival are clear enough; but the Romantic sources of Neo-classical architecture are perhaps less easily identified. The basis of Neo-classical architecture lay –

paradoxically perhaps – in a Romantic rebellion against the dying world of Renaissance tradition. Its idealist approach to purity of form, its fundamentalist belief in the unity of structure and decoration, its obsession with the primitive and the archaic, its ruthless dismissal of Palladian decorative conventions, its wilful disruption of the compositional rhythms of Baroque, its hint of megalomania – all these are expressions of Neo-classical architecture's Romantic foundation. Hence the invention by architectural historians of an alternative (and unnecessary) label: 'Romantic Classicism'. And hence the emergence of the Greek Revival – frequently in a naturalistic, Picturesque setting – as the climax of the whole Neo-classical movement in architecture.

Whatever their theoretical origins, however, it was the development of classical archaeology which made first Neo-classicism and then the Greek Revival possible. The rediscovery of ancient Greece during the eighteenth and early nineteenth centuries was the result of two complementary traditions of research, one French the other English. The French tradition began in the 1670s with the Levantine voyages of one ambassador, the Comte de Nointel, and one antiquarian of international repute, Jacob Spon. Soon afterwards Antoine Desgodets' *Édifices de Rome* (1682) established for the first time a methodology of architectural archaeology. But when this French tradition was resumed with Le Roy's *Ruines . . . de la Grèce* (1758) – under the influence of the Comte de Caylus, after a gap of more than half a century – leadership had already passed to the other side of the Channel. The English tradition had also begun in the 1670s with expeditions to Greece by Francis Vernon, Sir Giles Eastcourt and Sir George Wheler. It was continued in the 1730s and 1740s with the travels of men like Pococke, Rawdon and 'Palmyra' Wood, Richard Dalton (*Musaeum Graecum*, 1752), the Earl of Sandwich and the Earl of Charlemont. With the foundation of the Dilettanti Society in 1732, England captured the initiative. And English leadership was confirmed with the publication of 'Athenian' Stuart and Nicholas Revett's seminal *Antiquities of Athens* (1762; later volumes 1787, 1794, 1816 and

1830). During the next generation the French tradition produced little more than Dumont's *Paestum* (1769) and Normand's *Parallèle des Ordres* (1819). It was the English architectural archaeologists who led the field: Revett's *Ionian Antiquities* (1769 and 1797), Gandy and Bedford's *Unedited Antiquities of Attica* (1817), Wilkins's *Magna Graecia* (1807) and W. H. Inwood's *Erectheion* (1827) – to name only the most influential works. By comparison, the contribution of other countries was small. Winckelmann's *Observations on the Architecture of the Ancients* (1762) and *History of Ancient Art* (1764) established him as the German prophet of Greek Revivalism. But Winckelmann never visited Greece.

So the explanation and publication of Greek remains stemmed from the operation of two major traditions. Gallic fundamentalism and English empiricism joined forces in pursuit of the antique. The results, however, were slow in coming. Palladian tradition was still powerful. The progressive viewpoint was summed up by the *Critical Review* in 1759 when it described Sayer's edition of Le Roy as 'an attempt to restore architecture to its ancient dignity . . . enabling the beholder and reader to attain to the correct sublime in that noble art, after its having been so long mistaken'. But many, like Sir William Chambers, refused to be cheated 'into a Reverence for Attic deformity', believing 'they might with equal success oppose a Hottentot and a Baboon to the Apollo and the Gladiator as set up the Grecean Architecture against the Roman'. As a result, the Greek Revival did not dominate English, still less European, architecture until the end of the Napoleonic War. Still, the second half of the eighteenth century saw a gradual erosion of the Renaissance mystique. A new generation of Grand Tourists was looking beyond Rome to Greece. Before long Lord Byron and Lord Elgin would replace Lord Burlington. Even young Robert Adam, a hard-headed Scot bent on the creation of his own stylistic synthesis, felt the tug of Romantic Hellenism. In 1756, in a letter to his brother James, he expressed a sneaking wish 'to view the Temple[s] of Athens, of Thebes, of Sparta; the field of Marathon and Straits of Thermopyle, and though the Thought is altogether imaginary yet it is pleasing to be where harrangued Demosthenes, where fought Epaminondas and where Pericles counciled . . .' Five years later the fashion for archaeology was sufficiently established to be in danger of becoming a cliché: Hogarth impishly caricatured the pundits with his 'Five orders of PERRIWIGS . . . measured Architectonically . . . taken from the Statues, Bustos, and Baso-Relievos of Athens, Palmira, Balbec, and Rome'. And by 1791 Horace Walpole was being unfashionably *outré* in affecting to despise 'that ugly pigeon-house, the Temple of the Winds, that fly-cage, Demosthenes's lanthorn, and [other such] . . . fragments . . . or [pieces] . . . of . . . column crushed into a mud wall'. The leaven of Greek Revivalism had begun to operate. By 1808 a successful surburban architect, C. A. Busby, could remark: 'in almost all new buildings, Grecian members and ornaments are so prevalent as to obtrude themselves on the notice of the most superficial observer.' Harrison and Latrobe, Dance and Soane, Wilkins and Smirke, Basevi and Cockerell, Hamilton and Playfair – successive stages in the Hellenization of British architecture. A whole generation of future Royal Academicians grew up with Fuseli's war cry ringing in their ears: 'The Greeks were Gods!'

This, then, was the Neo-classical environment which Smirke inherited, the background against which his British Museum must be judged. The Greek Revival, as the climax of a movement historicist in origin readily took on museological form. The omnivorous quality of Neo-classical taste accorded happily with the museological mentality. Thomas Hope's 'temple of art' at Duchess Street, London (*c.* 1800) contained trophies of widely different origins – archaic, oriental, hellenistic and medieval. Sir John Soane's private museum in Lincoln's Inn Fields [30] was, and is, the perfect Neo-classical miscellany – in John Britton's words, *The Union of Architecture, Sculpture and Painting* (1827). Not surprisingly, the ultra-classical public museum, art gallery or library is perhaps the most typical expression of Greek Revivalism in architecture. Etymologically at least, the modern museum was an attempt to re-create the concept of an antique temple. Logically enough, architects attempted to re-create

30. Sir John Soane's Museum, London

the concept by reproducing the form. Hence the classic format of so much museum design. The Grecian columns of the British Museum can be matched – in style if not in number – in almost every capital city in the world.

In Britain alone the number of classical museums, art galleries and libraries must run into hundreds. During the Regency and Victorian periods, when the age of the great private patron overlapped with the age of municipal enterprise, temples of the arts proliferated in every city and county town. In 1800 there were less than a dozen public museums in the British Isles. By 1850 there were nearly sixty. By 1887 there were at least 240. And by 1928, 530. Many of these combined museum, picture gallery and library in one complex. Between 1800 and 1837, thirty-six museums were founded. These were mostly emanations of local learned societies – G. A. Underwood's Literary and Scientific Institution at Bath (1823–5) for example, or William Wilkins's Philosophical Society Museum at York (1827–30) – both gravely Doric. These buildings represented some of the best aspects of Regency provincial culture, particularly in the West Country and in the north. And their style was uniformly classical. But it was not in the old county towns that the big expansion of museums in the Victorian period occurred. The museological explosion of the later nineteenth century took place, quite rightly, in the new industrial centres – redressing the squalor of the new world with the wisdom and beauty of the old. Between 1850 and 1914 some 295 museums were founded in Britain, mostly in urban environments. And many of the buildings were completely new: about 90 between 1845 and 1914. This process was specifically assisted by legislation: the 1845 Museums Act; the 1850 Public Libraries (and museums) Act; the 1855 Free Library Act; the 1871 Museums and Gymnasiums Act; and the 1919 Public Libraries Act. The cumulative effect of this legislative process was to create a national network of museums, art galleries and libraries largely subsidized by local ratepayers. During the Victorian period the random distribution of these buildings seldom corresponded at all exactly to the distribution of population. A good deal depended on local initiative, private generosity and municipal pride. The private patron was still a crucial factor: Sir Andrew Walker and William Browne of Liverpool, Edmund Harris of Preston, William Atkinson of Stockport, Sir Joseph Whitworth of Manchester, John Bowes of Barnard Castle, John Newton Mappin of Sheffield – these are just a few of the patrons remembered eponymously up and down Britain. And then, of course, there was Andrew Carnegie and Sir Henry Tate. By no means all these buildings were classical. The Muses now had John Ruskin for an ally. But a clear majority maintained the classic tradition.

So the British Museum is only the best known of a long series of British museums and art galleries based on a modulated temple format. Half a dozen examples illustrate the point clearly enough: William Stark's short-lived Hunterian Museum in Glasgow (1804) [31], combining a central dome with porticoes in the primitive Tuscan style; Sir

31. The Hunterian Museum, Glasgow (1804), William Stark. Demolished 1865

32. City Art Gallery, Manchester (1823), Sir Charles Barry

33. Ashmolean Museum, Oxford (1841-5), C. R. Cockerell

Charles Barry's Royal Institution (later City Art Gallery) at Manchester (1823) [32], almost Parisian in feeling with its unfluted Ionic columns and smooth rustication; C. R. Cockerell's Ashmolean at Oxford (1841-5) [33], a highly personal fusion of Greek, Roman and Renaissance forms; George Basevi's Fitzwilliam Museum at Cambridge (1837-75; completed

34. Royal Scottish Academy (1822-6 and 1832-5), W. H. Playfair.

35. Fitzwilliam Museum, Cambridge (1837-75), George Basevi

by C. R. Cockerell and E. M. Barry) [35], with its mighty Corinthian portico in the Graeco-Roman manner; W. H. Playfair's twin temples in the heart of Edinburgh, 'the Athens of the North' – the Royal Scottish Academy (1822-6 and 1832-5) [34] and Scottish National Gallery (1850-57) – Doric and Ionic respectively; and, late enough to merit the label

'Greek Re-Revival', the Harris Free Library, Museum and Art Gallery at Preston, Lancashire (1882–93) [36], designed in a provincial version of *beaux arts* classicism by an accomplished local Hellenist, James Hibbert. The element of continuity – between Wilkins's National Gallery in Trafalgar Square (1832–8) [37] and Smith's Tate Gallery on Millbank

36. Harris Free Library, Museum and Art Gallery, Preston (1882–93), J. Hibbert

(1897) [38] – is clear enough. The 'temple of the arts' remains a dominant museological concept throughout the nineteenth century, broken only briefly by the popularity of Ruskinian Gothic in the High Victorian period.

37. National Gallery, London (1832-8), William Wilkins

Such is the museological context into which Smirke's British Museum must be fitted. Its place in the architectural typology of the Regency is clear enough. But what were the architectural principles governing its design? In 1846, Smirke's pupil C. R. Cockerell – the prince of British classicists, then at the height of his powers – wrote to his old tutor as follows: 'My dear maestro . . . you are . . . truly the grandfather of all my productions.' Fortunately, Smirke's approach to classical design is excellently documented. For if we wish to understand our maestro's music, we must first listen patiently while he explains his method of composition.

38. Tate Gallery, London (1897), Sydney Smith

Smirke's philosophy of architecture is contained in a series of manuscript fragments preserved in the R.I.B.A. library in London. Random watermarks and scraps of internal evidence suggest that the essay was begun in 1815 and extensively revised over the next ten years with a view to publication. Its language is occasionally pompous and its digressive structure benefits from drastic pruning and rearrangement. But although Smirke apologizes for 'the . . . brevity and slight texture of this . . . hasty sketch', its historical importance is considerable. On the whole Regency architects published little in the way of architectural theory. Thomas Sandby's Royal Academy lectures have survived in manuscript; those of Soane and C. R. Cockerell are available in print. But George Dance neither lectured nor published, nor did Nash, nor did any of the pre-Victorian Wyatts.

Apart from its obvious rarity, Smirke's treatise is intrinsically interesting as a doctrinaire expression of Neo-classicism. His admiration for Greek architecture is intense. 'On turning over the vast collection of that ingenious and indefatigable raker of antiquities, Piranesi', he finds no more than 'a monument . . . of corrupt [Roman] taste.' The Grecian style he considered 'the noblest' of all possible styles: 'simple, grand, magnificent without ostentation, and everywhere discovering a rational purpose effected by the best means . . . a style which [Nature might have chosen] had nature provided . . . edifices for man's use. . . . [For] with its other merits it has a kind of primal simplicity. . . . An excess of ornament is in all cases a sympton of a vulgar or degenerate taste.' Greek architecture, he believed, had degenerated in Roman hands 'till its despicable remains were almost everywhere superseded by that singular and mysterious compound of styles' known as Gothic. 'Hence were derived the steeples, towers, pinnacles, balconies, balustrades and other features' of Renaissance design.

Smirke's admiration for Grecian buildings did not, however, turn him into an unthinking copyist. Unlike William Wilkins, he is more concerned with theory than with archaeology. He concentrates on principles rather than on precedents, leaving 'the learned labour . . . of the anti-quary' to 'the idle or the curious'. His standpoint is that of a disciple of Cordemoy, Laugier and Blondel. His thinking forms part of the main-stream of French rationalist theory. Thanks to his training under Dance and Soane, thanks to his assimilation of Continental attitudes during the Napoleonic period, his adherence to the fundamentalist philosophy of Laugier's *Essai sur l'Architecture* (1753) and *Observations sur l'Architecture* (1765) is more dogmatic and complete than that of any other British architectural writer. His unpublished treatise explodes his textbook reputation as a scholarly, archaeologically-minded architect. He is re-vealed as a romantic functionalist. The theme is structural integrity rather than decorative accuracy. And on the basis of this critical appara-tus, he confidently dismisses the whole of Renaissance architecture as 'debased'. Palladio, Inigo Jones, Wren, Vanbrugh, Burlington, Gibbs – all stand condemned, convicted of gross impurity and habitual falsity.

Palladio . . . thought only of purifying the different orders. . . . Hence [his] buildings . . . seem not so much *composed* of the materials they exhibit, as to be hung round with them. . . . The boasted Parisian buildings are chiefly of this description. . . . The Tuileries, the Louvre and Palais Royale. . . . [Similarly, Inigo Jones's Banqueting House in Whitehall] is richly hung with architectural *paper* . . . exhibiting a spacious, but false show of . . . beams . . . that in better times were accustomed to give proofs of real usefulness. . . . The double range of columnar ghosts . . . intersected by successive courses of entablatures, checker and divide it into square compartments . . . [producing a design] in which the forms of architecture are spread for no purpose that might not, with equal advantage, be answered by their . . . painted simulations. . . . [This] basso relievo style [has given birth to] . . . much that is ingenious, little that is good, and a prodigious mass of what is execrable . . .

. . . [St Peter's Rome and St Paul's London] are both in the same impure taste, so that it would be difficult to determine which is the least defective . . . [As for] Sir John Vanbrugh . . . *Heaviness* was the lightest of his faults. . . . The Italian style . . . which he contrived to caricature . . . is apparent in all his works; he helped himself liberally to its vices, contributed many of his own, and by an unfortunate misfortune, adding impurity to that which was already greatly impure, left it disgusting and often odious. . . . [Lord Burlington was] an architectural genius. . . . Let the Romans who corrupted the Greek, and the Italians who still further corrupted the Roman art, bear the weight of his professional sins . . . The Chiswick villa, though an architectural gew-gaw . . . ranks among the least faulty compositions of a school in which error is sanctioned and systematically taught . . . [After] Burlington [English] . . . architecture . . . just existed . . . and taste [became a matter of pattern books] . . . Published materials [enabled] . . . the most ordinary man . . . to stumble upon designs of a superior quality . . . [James Gibb's] St Martin-in-the-Fields is probably a casualty of this kind [for] St Mary-le-Strand is in everything the complete opposite . . .

From this state of degradation, Smirke believed, architecture was rescued by the Greek Revival. The rediscovery of Grecian antiquities purged and purified architectural design – not by exchanging one decorative scheme for another, but by redefining the principles of architectural composition.

If Greek orders are displayed exactly as Italian ones were before . . . there is no real difference between Italianised Roman and Grecianised Italian . . . In fact, if *composition* be not reformed and purged of its Italian impurities, every new importation of the scraps and rakings of Greek remains, only expose the art to dangers of the most serious nature . . . Let . . . the *style of composition* . . . be restored to its original purity, and it matters little . . . what may be its decorations . . . or whether its orders be more or less exactly imitated.

What therefore is the key to the recovery of true purity? In effect, Smirke puts forward a single aesthetic panacea: Laugier's doctrine of 'apparent utility'.

When useful members of an edifice are introduced ornamentally . . . they should *appear* . . . to have a possible utility, and . . . be placed only in situations where they would seem natural and necessary . . . Whether [Laugier's] idea of the simple primeval cottage as the origin of the Greek system, be true or false, it affords an explanation that carries with it irresistable conviction . . . [a] *standard* to be constantly referred to . . . [For example] an ARCHITRAVE . . . when broken . . . is no longer an architrave . . . [and] the well-instructed eye . . . will not tolerate an affection of *infirmity* . . . The PORTICO [should] . . . appear to be either actually useful, or not evidently otherwise; and it is on this ground of *apparent utility* that it chiefly claims our respect . . . There is no principle of taste more unquestionable than the impertinence of useless columns . . . [COLON-NADES should] afford . . . shelter . . . [from] the sweeping torrent or scorching sun-beams . . . [But instead they] have gradually shrunk into the walls behind them, until their architraves refuse shade even to the swallows that would fain build their nests below; . . . the columns . . . [leave] only their spectres on the surface . . . [as] pilasters which might have been applied . . . by the hand of the painter. There is indeed something approaching to moral turpitude . . . in such flimsy daubings of superficial finery . . . The immersion of columns into . . . walls [is another example] of depraved art, but a defect still more preposterous is the gradual shrinking of . . . [a portico] into the parts behind it, leaving only the faint traces of its general conformation, as if to mark the grave where it lies interred! . . . PILASTERS [constitute] a show of strength as unnecessary as it is untrue . . . The BALUSTRADE . . . can rarely have the sanction of real or apparent utility . . . If employed merely as decoration, it is a common and vulgar expedient . . . The NICHE . . . is a monstrous conceit . . . a useless *hole in the wall* [which] merits a distinguished place on the list of architectural absurdities . . . RUSTICA-TION . . . is an old and incorrigible imposter . . . a really and apparently useless deformity: being a positive imitation of that which is truly an imperfection . . . [Even] the CORINTHIAN CAPITAL . . . a [mere] *bundle of leaves* . . . a *bouquet* masking the architrave with an affectation of support [is permissible only in] interior architecture . . . [Even] the IONIC ORDER [with its] unintelligible trinkets [is suspect] . . . [Even] the CARYATID . . . is . . . one of those crimes in art which has no other claim to our indulgence than its antiquity . . . [For] it is a monstrous incongruity to give *efficient* offices to ornamental details . . . The tea-pot in the shape of a swan, although a more elegant form, is of the same barbarous taste as the well-known ale pitcher in that of Toby Philpot. The hinder legs of goats converted into the supporters of a stool or tripod is an ancient abomina-tion; and to compose the feet of tables . . . of the *paws* of the lion, or of the eagle's *claws*, is a vice of the same quality . . . Bundles of reeds as Roman fasces usurping the place of columns; marble Naiades with streaming urns, and sea-nymphs and sea-horses, on a fountain, all dissolving in liquid crystal; the heads of animals ranged on a cornice with open mouths prepared to eject the falling shower, these and a thousand other conceits are all either ancient or modern pollutions of art.

Laugier's doctrine was indeed a mighty purge. No wonder C. R. Cockerell called Smirke 'provokingly rational'. At one blow the whole rationale of Renaissance classicism seemed to crumble. But even though it was buoyed up by the strength of so much Gallic logic, in the long run the foundations of Neo-classical theory proved equally insecure. The doctrine of 'apparent utility' itself embodied a fiction: columns and architraves must look *as if* they supported something. This fiction of decoration 'as if' has been nicely described by Sir John Summerson as 'subjunctive architecture'. Smirke sums it all up with a parable about a lame man whose crutches are compared to classical columns: 'after being cured of his lameness, should he still choose to carry his wooden props about with him . . . he would deserve the ridicule that would certainly follow so absurd a conceit. If he must needs carry his crutches . . . he should at least *affect* to be lame.' But how long could architects keep up such a pretence? How tolerable were even the most elegant crutches after the patient had learnt to walk? It is precisely this affectation of rationality which makes some of the premises of Neo-classical architecture so hard to swallow. After all, Smirke's Greek Revival buildings – including the British Museum – were structurally independent of their masonry dressing: they depended in fact on cast iron and concrete.

Nevertheless, if we can accept the disciplinary and linguistic functions of the revived Grecian style – and we must, if we are ever to understand Neo-classicism – then the intellectual credentials of Greek Revivalism have a certain closed-circuit validity. Smirke's treatise implicitly admits the fictional quality of much Greek Revival architecture. But it also indicates just how far the movement could emancipate itself from archaeology.

And that brings us to the crux of the Neo-classical dilemma: the battle between archaeology and experimentalism. Brought up by Dance and Soane in the Cordemoy-Laugier tradition, Smirke believed the architect had a twofold function: to rediscover pure classical forms and to adapt them to new circumstances. Of course, both functions – historicism and rationalism – pulled in opposite directions. That was the trouble. And Smirke recognized the problem even if he failed to solve it. He was more concerned with the fundamentals than with the details of architectural composition. Anti-Baroque and anti-Palladian, his most significant designs assume a disparate, geometrical form consonant with the ethos of the Picturesque. 'Rectangular shapes', he wrote, are 'the component materials of every modern work.' Pugin called it 'the New Square Style of Mr Smirke'. It was an architecture of understatement, poised precariously between promise and platitude. For, above all, Smirke scorned architectural transvestism: the mere translation of Roman into Greek. Like Schinkel he dreamed of building 'as the Greeks would have built had they lived now'. The Regency had a word for Smirke's architectural simplicity. They called it 'chastity'. Adam and Wyatt had not been entirely chaste. Vanbrugh, Wren and Hawksmoor had been positively sinful. But Smirke carried chastity to unprecedented lengths. Nash and Soane were never able to maintain quite the same standard of visual morality.

Unfortunately Smirke was too prolific to live up to his own ideals. The promise of Covent Garden Theatre was not fulfilled. In its emphasis on geometrical forms, its juxtaposition of blocks independently conceived, its almost cubic simplicity, Covent Garden embodied that transition from Baroque coherence to Picturesque disparity which was the very basis of Neo-classicism. Unhappily for English architecture, however, it was the paraphernalia of revivalism, rather than the compositional possibilities of the new idiom which won immediate recognition. And, unfortunately for Smirke's reputation, he spent the remainder of his career catering for the market he had helped to create. The Greek Revival in England, if not in Scotland, declined into a series of stylized clichés: the purity of Dance, Soane and Smirke gave way to the Grecian villas of J. C. Loudon's *Encyclopaedia* (1833). Historicism triumphed over rationalism. Four of Smirke's classical country houses – Kinmount (1812), Whittinghame (1818), Luton Hoo (1816 onwards; much rebuilt),

39. Normanby Park, Lincolnshire (1821), Sir Robert Smirke

and Normanby Park (1821) [39] – go some way towards coining what might almost be described as a Graeco-cubic style. Contemporaries sometimes simply called it 'modern'. But in most cases, decoration from the Ilissus temple, the Theseion or the Erechtheion is merely grafted on to Georgian stock. His largest buildings, the General Post Office, the British Museum, the Custom House, and King's College, London, all embody conventions which are unmistakably Palladian. In this way his enormous influence channelled the development of the Greek Revival away from the fertile experimentalism of Dance and Soane, and into the arid wastes of copyism.

But if Smirke failed to solve the Neo-classical dilemma, at least he failed in good company. The real lesson to be drawn from his career is not so much stylistic as psychological: the corrupting effect of success. Quite simply, the quality of his work suffered from over-production. When in 1818, along with Nash and Soane, he was invited by the Church Commissioners to send in specimen church designs, he produced a striking prototype in his best Graeco-cubic manner. But his executed versions were all rather more perfunctory. In less than four years (1821–5), seven Commissioners' churches were built to his designs, one Gothic and six classic. Of these five – three Ionic: St Mary, Bryanston Square, St Anne, Wandsworth, and St Philip, Salford; and two Doric: St James, West Hackney, and St George, Bristol – boast an almost identical 'pepper-pot' steeple. And this steeple was not even the architect's own invention, but an adaptation of one of Stephen Riou's ideas, published in *Grecian . . . Architecture . . . Explained* (1768). There is a solemn predictability about much of Smirke's work which deadens criticism. As the *Athenaeum* remarked in 1843, 'Sir Robert Smirke . . . is always respectable – and no more: never absolutely shocks, and never captivates'.

In many ways Smirke was too much of a professional to be an artist, too busy to be original. Schiller put it more poetically:

> The artist is the son of his time;
> Happy for him if he is not its pupil,
> And happier still if he is not its favourite.

4: The New British Museum

'One of the finest compositions of modern times'
(Professor T. L. Donaldson, 1867)

'An absurdity' (James Fergusson, 1862)

When Smirke joined the Office of Works in 1815, schemes for extending or reconstructing the British Museum had been in the air for more than a decade. And so rapid was the museum's expansion that work continued long after his retirement in 1846. Smirke's rebuilding of the British Museum should therefore be understood as part of a continuous historical process, extending over half a century. Such an organic approach helps to resolve an initial difficulty with regard to the museum's architectural history. For at the outset historians are faced with a problem of chronology. What relation, if any, does the design of the museum bear to the designs of contemporary Continental museums? What was the date of its conception? Is it a precedent, a copy or an independent production?

Attempts have been made to place Smirke's design more exactly in its European context, and these attempts have meant the postdating of a major part of the design by no less than thirteen years. In brief, it has been argued that the dramatic conception of the entrance front [40] dates not from 1823 when the original plans were officially approved, nor from 1833 when these plans were modified for the sake of economy, but from 1836 when they were first published in diagrammatic form. Now the British Museum certainly formed part of a general European movement, that alliance between the cult of the antique and the fashion for organized *Kultur*, which produced a rash of museum-building during the post-Napoleonic period. But a strict examination of the genesis and chron-

40 *(above)*. The British Museum (1823), Sir Robert Smirke

41 *(opposite above)*. The Glyptothek, Munich (1816–30), Leo von Klenze

42 *(opposite)*. The Altes Museum, Berlin (designed 1823, built 1825–8), K. F. Schinkel

ology of Smirke's scheme reveals that the design was almost certainly conceived with no more than indirect reference to its Continental counter-parts, Klenze's Glyptothek in Munich (1816–30) [41] and Schinkel's Altes Museum in Berlin (designed 1823, built 1825–8) [42].

In 1802 George III's presentation of the Egyptian antiquities captured at Alexandria prompted the Trustees to set up a buildings committee

consisting of Sir Joseph Banks, Sir William Hamilton, Thomas Astle and Charles Townley. Their report, presented in the following year, laid down the pattern of the museum's future growth. They recommended a programme of staggered expansion with galleries running northwards from the main building first to the west and then to the east of the garden behind Montagu House. Here was the genesis of a new British Museum. It was this programme which was begun by Saunders in 1804 and expanded by Smirke from 1816 onwards. Saunders prepared three different proposals: two Palladian, and one in the style of Montagu House [21]. The larger Palladian version was chosen. From the start, therefore, no attempt was made to imitate the architecture of the original building. Saunders's Townley Gallery survived as a Palladian anachronism surrounded by Smirke's new Grecian work until 1846.

The purchase of the Phigaleian and Elgin Marbles in 1815-16 underlined the need for expansion. Their arrival also coincided with the museum's inclusion under the umbrella of the Office of Works. The stage seemed set for full-scale rebuilding. But immediate needs were met by a very temporary measure - a prefabricated Elgin Gallery.

Since Lord Elgin's return to England in 1806 his priceless collection had been stored in the houses of the Duchess of Portland and the Duke of Richmond and then exhibited to the cognoscenti of the metropolis 'in a damp dirty penthouse' at No. 6 Park Lane. Here they were examined and admired by Haydon, Lawrence, West, Flaxman, Fuseli, Hamilton, Knight, Smirke and many others. In 1812 another eighty cases of marbles arrived in London. After prevarication by the government and opposition from the egregious Payne Knight – who believed most of them Hadrianic – the marbles were reluctantly paid for by the Treasury. Meanwhile, as an interim compromise, Royal Academy students were permitted to sketch them at Burlington House. With help from Flaxman, Westmacott and a marble cutter named Pistol, Smirke designed two prefabricated rooms [59] to the west of the Townley Gallery. 'Con-

structed of frame work with fir timber and single bricks', they cost
£2,500. Despite the risk of fire and its increasingly 'decaying state', this
curious structure enshrined the Elgin and Phigaleian Marbles until 1831.
And it was here – amid rough timbers and cast iron ties – that young John
Keats first felt a 'dizzy pain' as he gazed upon 'these mighty things', and
marvelled how they mingled 'Grecian grandeur with the rude Wasting
of old Time'.

In the euphoric years after Waterloo there was some talk of rebuilding
the British Museum on a new site – in Waterloo Place in fact, on the site
of Carlton House. But nothing came of the idea. Instead, in 1820, the
Trustees revived their programme of 1803 and directed Smirke to begin
collecting information as to the museum's requirements. For this purpose he went to several senior members of the museum staff: Sir Henry
Ellis, Sir Joseph Planta, Taylor Combe and Edward Hawkins. He also
took advice from the Trustees' advisory committee: Sir Joseph Banks,
Sir Charles Long (later Lord Farnborough), 'Athenian' Aberdeen, Lord
Spencer, Lord Seymour and Richard Payne Knight. These were the men
who supplied instructions as to the museum's present and future needs,
and they – as much as the architect – must share any blame for the inadequacy of the eventual design. In February 1821, on behalf of the Trustees,
Smirke recommended to the Treasury the erection of two parallel wings
to the north of Montagu House. Preparation of detailed estimates began
at once. But final plans were held up for nearly two years by negotiations
with the Bedford estate. And by the time permission had been secured
the project had assumed a new urgency: George IV's transfer of his
father's library in January 1823 turned the projected east wing into the
King's Library, the first stage of Smirke's grand design.

From the start, financial stringency meant that this grand design was
envisaged in the form of a piecemeal building programme. The plan of
the new British Museum was superimposed on the layout of Montagu
House. As one went up, the other came down – in stages. In 1823 all the

interested parties – architect, Treasury and Trustees – agreed to the same long-term plan:

The three sides of the quadrangle might be built and occupied while the central apartments of the present house and the wings containing the apartments of the officers continue to stand, and the quadrangle could be completed according to the designs, when it became desirable or necessary to take down these old buildings . . . [The King's Library] should evidently form part of an entire plan, for the present edifice . . . is in a decaying state . . . The existing building would not interfere with such a general design; it would be appropriated to its present uses until the various objects contained in it were gradually removed into the new edifice.

The quadrangular form lent itself naturally to a programme of staggered development. It also suited the Bloomsbury site. Montagu House, its forecourt and garden, together constituted a rectangular strip of land with only one opening – towards Great Russell Street. On its other three sides the area was hemmed in by the property of the Bedford estate. Such an introverted site made the adoption of an open quadrangle logical and necessary.

So much for the circumstances of Smirke's commission. What of the chronology of his design? And how much is known about its stylistic origins?

While still a student at the Royal Academy, Smirke had tried his hand at multi-columned schemes in the French *Grand Prix* tradition. Such exercises in stylophily were *de rigueur* for Neo-classical neophytes throughout Europe. But by freezing their prize-winning designs in published form, the French Academy of Architecture had established an international reputation in this particular field. Smirke's practice projects were adapted from designs by his tutor, George Dance Jr, and made liberal use of massive columnar screens. One such design probably dates from *c*. 1798-9, twelve years before the French architectural theorist J. N. L. Durand published a similar columnar paradigm in his seminal *Leçons d'Architecture* [50]. In 1797 young Smirke produced 'designs for a

Square and a Palace proposed to be built in Hyde Park'. And in 1799 he won the Royal Academy Gold Medal with a 'Design for a National Museum'. Both these schemes reflect the Parisian influence transmitted via Dance, and both anticipate the columnar characteristics of his later elevations for the British Museum. Given his training and taste, Smirke found himself, inevitably, within the mainstream of European aesthetics. His British Museum, in form and decoration, naturally bears the impress of European Neo-classicism. In 1779 the French Academy of Architecture had chosen 'A Museum' as their competition theme, and both winning designs – by Gisors and Delannoy [43] – had adopted a basically

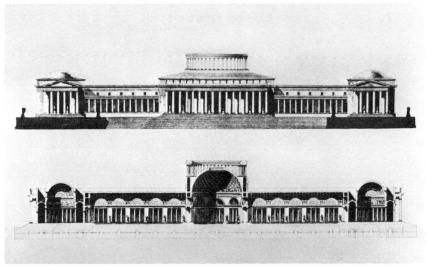

43. Grand Prix Design for a Museum (1779), Delannoy

quadrangular form. But neither is the source of Smirke's design. We must look elsewhere.

The composition of Smirke's façade – the projecting wings, the 'centre and ends' arrangement – rests firmly on the traditions of British Palladianism. And at this point a convincing source naturally springs to

44, 45. The Parliament House, Dublin (1729 onwards), Sir Edward Lovett Pearce
A. House of Commons
B. House of Lords
C. Court of Requests

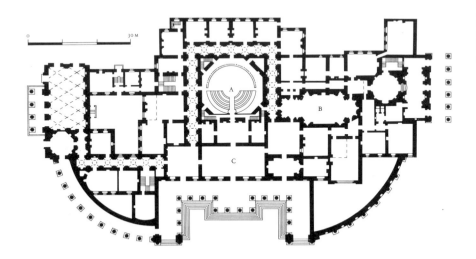

mind: the Parliament House in Dublin [44, 45], now the Bank of Ireland, begun in 1728 to designs by Vanbrugh's cousin, Sir Edward Lovett Pearce (*c.* 1699–1733), and later completed by James Gandon, Robert Parke and Francis Johnston. Compositionally speaking, the suggestion is unimpeachable: Smirke seems merely to have expanded the theme of Pearce's articulated colonnade, and changed the order from Roman Ionic to Greek. We know that in 1767 the Parliament House was fully published in plan, elevation and section. And, better still, Dr Maurice Craig has discovered that an engraving of Pearce's design was produced by Thomas Malton in 1792 – with figures by Robert Smirke Sr [45].

But such a solution to the conundrum seemed almost too simple, certainly too insular, for international scholars to accept without a struggle. Might not Schinkel and Klenze be drawn into the picture? With this objective in mind, Sir Nikolaus Pevsner set himself the task of relating the British Museum to those in Berlin and Munich. There was only one stumbling-block: the traditional date of design – 1823. If it could be proved that Smirke's colonnade was not in fact the product of that year but a later postscript or after-thought, then Bloomsbury's pioneer status would be somewhat diminished. After all, was it possible that such a dull architect as Smirke could lead where Klenze and Schinkel followed? Hence the attempt – begun by Pevsner and pursued by Professor Henry-Russell Hitchcock – to rearrange the chronology of Smirke's design. But it was an attempt based on the flimsiest evidence. In brief, the suggestion that Smirke's great entrance front was designed not in 1823 but in 1836, and was therefore susceptible to several intermediary precedents, can only be substantiated by making light of iconographical and testimentary evidence and by leaning heavily on the suspect reporting of a gossip column for dilettanti.

In 1824 this periodical – *The Somerset House Gazette and Literary Museum: or weekly miscellany of fine arts, antiquities and Literary Chit-Chat*, edited by Ephraim Hardcastle [W. H. Pyne] – published a rumour that the new museum was to follow the precedent of Somerset House: a quadrangle pierced by a vaulted entrance carriageway, a quotation borrowed in turn by Sir William Chambers from the Farnese Palace in Rome and hardly palatable to a Greek Revivalist like Smirke. *The Times* printed the story, but followed it a few weeks later with Smirke's official programme, itemizing a piecemeal quadrangular plan, an elaboration of the programmes of 1803 and 1821. It was this scheme for progressive reconstruction which was presented to the Treasury in July 1823, and to the members of a select Parliamentary committee at about the same time, before being lodged with the Trustees. Tenders for the first stage were accepted in the autumn.

Now, despite changes in 1833, this general plan remained unpublished until 1836. The entrance elevation was not published until 1844. Even official access was limited to a specially prepared scale model, located from about 1830 onwards in the old Trustees' Room in Montagu House, and now apparently lost. This secrecy seems to have stemmed, at least in part, from Smirke's natural reticence. He was known for his hauteur, his dignified indifference, his 'talent for silence'. In true eighteenth-century fashion, he regarded architectural composition as a private matter between architect and patron, 'utterly unintelligible to the vulgar'. He not only never published his works in the press, he never exhibited designs at the Royal Academy – only restorations of antique remains. His attitude became so notorious that he was once christened the Royal Academy's 'Absent Member'. He was, however, quite correct in believing that the museum's grand entrance front could not be 'very satisfactorily shown in a drawing'; and he rightly preferred 'reference to be made to the model'. But as press speculation grew, and as pirated versions of his design began to appear, he was forced to break silence in 1844 and published an official lithograph [46] – as Sir Henry Ellis remarked, so 'that the snarkers may at least be quelled, if they cannot be satisfied'. That killed speculation at the time. But it has not killed speculation since. Was the elevation in the 1844 lithograph really the same as the elevation sanctioned in 1823?

46. Smirke's final design for the British Museum

In the spring of 1844, while defending his protégé against public criticism, Sir Robert Peel, then Prime Minister, assured the House of Commons that the entrance front of the museum, then in process of construction, had never been altered, but exactly followed the design originally authorized twenty years previously. Six years later Sir Robert Inglis repeated this statement in his evidence before a Parliamentary Commission. Peel had been Home Secretary in 1823, and both he and Inglis were Trustees of the museum, sitting on the Parliamentary committee of 1838 which investigated the building programme. Inglis was also for some years a member of the Trustees' sub-committee on buildings. But apart from their authors' experience, there are other persuasive reasons for accepting these statements.

We know that a provisional masterplan was drawn up and authorized in 1823. Several different proposals may well have been submitted in preliminary form. But no drawings or specifications survive to substantiate the 'Somerset House' rumour of the broken quadrangle. Instead

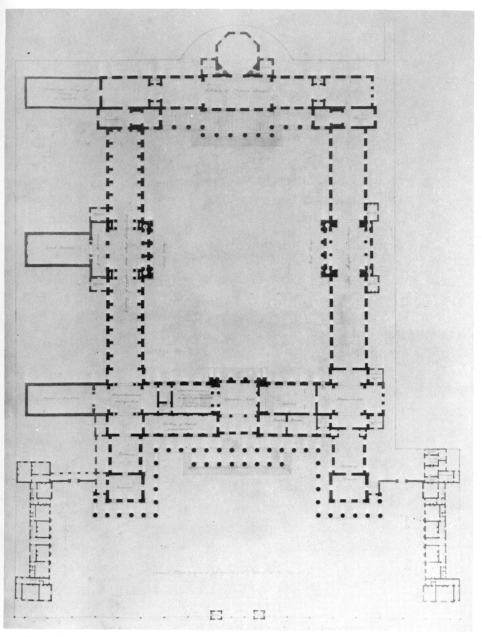

47. Ground plan of the British Museum (1827), Sir Robert Smirke

we have a number of drawings by Smirke in the Public Record Office, in the British Museum, in the R.I.B.A. and in private hands. They include one set of plans dated June 1827 [47], showing the colonnade in its final form. Several more are variously watermarked 1822, 1823 and 1825. These show schemes for the entrance and quadrangle elevations. The date of one undated drawing for the interior of the quadrangle is beyond dispute – 1823: the design follows another [48] dated '8th July 1823', and

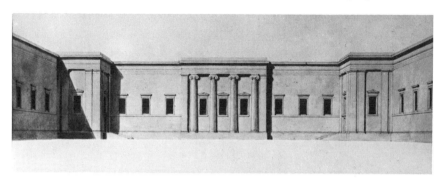

48. Design for the interior of the quadrangle of the British Museum (1823), Sir Robert Smirke

a third dated 1836 but inscribed 'according to the arrangement of the general plan made in 1823'. The watermark (1822) of another undated drawing showing a preliminary scheme very similar to the final entrance front must be granted at least *prima facie* acceptability. Like its signed duplicate [49], it is undated. But there is no stylistic reason for doubting

49. Smirke's first design for the British Museum (1823)

that both formed part of the provisional scheme presented to the Treasury in 1823. Elements of the final entrance front are clearly visible in Smirke's unexecuted design for the north side of the courtyard and in his various elevations for the exactly contemporary General Post Office (1823–9). The final form of the museum entrance front can be traced to these experiments with colonnades and porticoes in 1821–3, which in turn derive from the architect's early training under George Dance and perhaps from a visit to Dublin in 1817. Similarly, the quadrangular plan, rectangular rather than square, can be traced to *ad hoc* decisions by the Trustees dating back to 1803 and to the advice of museum officials in the period of gestation, 1821–3. In particular, according to W. R. Hamilton's testimony, it was Sir Joseph Banks who demanded 'a simple quadrangle, with four rooms below and four rooms above, large oblong galleries'. Finally, one crucial item of evidence clinches the argument. In August 1823, Smirke took advice as to the façade's design from his ablest pupil, C. R. Cockerell. Cockerell made a note of the meeting in his diary – and obligingly inserted a sketch plan of the great colonnade.

All in all, the evidence indicates firstly that in 1821 work began on a general plan which was finished early in 1823; secondly that this took the form of a closed quadrangle variously embellished with internal and external colonnades; and thirdly that in its essentials this scheme remained unaltered.

So much for attempts to fix the date 1836 on the entrance front of the British Museum. As for the suggestion of plagiarism, Smirke answered this question, slightly equivocally, before the Parliamentary committee of that year. He admitted examining the designs of other museums and libraries during the preparation of his own plans in 1821–3. 'But there are none of the same description', he claimed, 'in regard to the . . . extent and variety of the collections . . . , and some of the best were not then built. The great buildings at Berlin and Munich were not then erected. . . .

The only library I had seen possessing any character of architectural importance was the Imperial Library at Vienna, which is a room about 230 feet long and more expressive and magnificent in its decoration than any room in the museum here.' Now Schinkel's Altes Museum in Berlin [42] and Klenze's Pinakothek in Munich were certainly not built in 1823. But Klenze's Glyptothek at Munich [41] was begun in 1816. However, it lacks the columnar characteristics of Smirke's design. And even its quadrangular plan can have been no more significant in the genesis of its British equivalent than the circumstances of the Bloomsbury site. The common ancestor of all these designs, Durand's paradigm

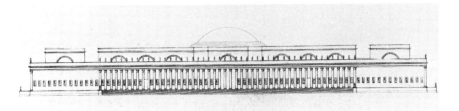

50. Design for a museum (1809), J. N. L. Durand

of 1809 [50], is at most indirect. Years later W. R. Hamilton recalled that not too much but too little attention had been paid to contemporary Continental museums.

The British Museum was essentially British in its conception. Its architect was by no means insular, but he borrowed the idea of the great colonnade not from a German but from an Irishman. And he derived the idea of the great forecourt and quadrangle not from the Farnese Palace, nor even from the visions of the French *grands prix*, but from a series of topographical accidents.

Finally, what was the source of Smirke's mighty Ionic order? Here again, the answer is by no means simple. Smirke's Neo-classicism was a synthetic style. Not surprisingly, therefore, the columns of the colon-

51. Detail of the portico of the British Museum

52 *(opposite)*. Ionic capital used in the quadrangle of the British Museum

nade [51, 52, 55] have no single antique source. The order is basically a modified version of that belonging to the Ionic temple of Athena Polias at Priene in Asia Minor [53, 54]. This had been illustrated in detail in the Dilettanti Society's volume *Ionian Antiquities* (1769). But Smirke has simplified the entablature and given the columns Attic bases instead of Asiatic ones. In this respect his model could have been the Temple of Dionysus at Teos [56], illustrated in the same volume. The temple at Priene also inspired the order of Smirke's contemporary General Post Office. But elsewhere – as for example at the Royal College of Physicians [29] – he made use of the simpler order illustrated in Stuart and Revett's first volume and usually known as the Ilissus Ionic.

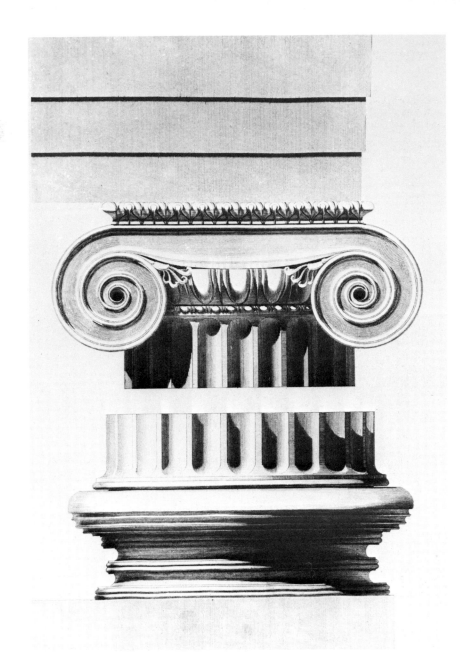

53. The temple of Athena Polias at Priene in Asia Minor: profile of column

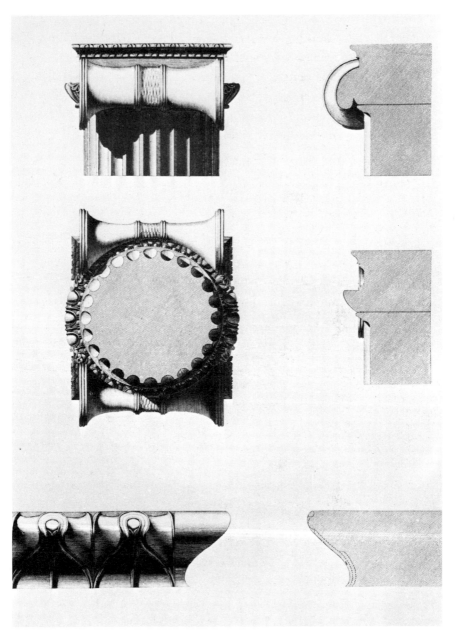

54. The temple of Athena Polias at Priene in Asia Minor: detail of capital

Although Smirke's original plan remained substantially unaltered, the elevations underwent two minor, but significant, changes. Until 1833 he intended the main quadrangle façades to carry fairly elaborate porticoes. Visitors would enter the giant entrance colonnade, pass through the entrance hall and emerge from a second portico facing into the open quadrangle. To enter the northern wing they would then cross the quadrangle, mount an imposing flight of steps and pass through another portico, the third. Smirke surrendered his original scheme 'with great regret', but he 'had the satisfaction to hear that both Lord Grey [the Prime Minister] and the Lord Chancellor [Lord Cottenham] expressed

55 *(below)*. Base of one of the columns in the portico of the British Museum

56 *(opposite)*. The temple of Dionysus at Teos: profile of column

the same regret'. Economy and lack of space reduced the two internal porticoes from majestic to decorative proportions. The same reasons ruled out the possibility of a linking corridor along the north wing, despite arguments based on coherence and convenience. For all its size – it was bigger than Hanover Square – the central area turned out to be useless for botanical purposes. Far from stimulating 'a free circulation of air', it became noisome and foetid – 'a mere well of malaria, a pestilent congregation of vapours'. In fact financial and climatic conditions quickly reduced Smirke's great quadrangle to the status of a gigantic white elephant. Thus, at a Parliamentary committee in 1836:

MR HAWES: When will the public have a view of the architecture of the inner quadrangle?

SIR ROBERT SMIRKE: When they are in the quadrangle.

Unfortunately few visitors shared the architect's confidence in the English weather. The quadrangle remained closed, visible only through a single glazed panel in a subsidiary door in the entrance hall. And in 1852 it was at last agreed that the area be filled in to form the Round Reading Room. All in all, the great quadrangle only existed in its finished form for seven years – from 1847 to 1854.

The other point of departure from Smirke's original elevations was the alteration of the entrance front during the 1840s. It originally echoed the General Post Office in its lack of ornamental sculpture and in its continuous plain parapet. There was even some intention to repeat the postal prototype even to the extent of placing the royal arms, a little incongruously, over the museum's doorway. But as the emphasis on the quadrangle diminished in 1833, so that on the entrance front proportionately increased. More important, perhaps, fashion was changing. And Smirke may have thought it discreet to bend a little to the prevailing aesthetic wind. Critics in the press, blindly speculating on the secret design, may well have persuaded him, between 1842 and 1844, to go some way towards meeting the early Victorian demand for 'significant' decoration.

Anyway, his earlier severity was modified by several new proposals: the modification of the string course, the enrichment of the central entrance, the inflection of the parapet and the inclusion of sculpture within the pediment and upon its apex and corners, sculptured groups flanking the steps, and sculptured friezes adorning the centre and wings [46].

These proposals would certainly have livened up the façade: the *Wrestlers* and the *Laocoön* were to have greeted visitors as they climbed the steps. It was T. L. Donaldson's opinion that these suggested additions would have set the seal on 'one of the finest compositions of modern times'. But of these proposals only three were put into effect: the alteration of the doorway and string course, the rhythmic variation of the parapet and the insertion of Richard Westmacott's pedimental sculpture, *The Progress of Civilisation*. Westmacott had 'a horror of appearing in print', but agreed to produce a description of his sculpture which was later expanded by Sir Henry Ellis:

> Commencing at the Eastern end . . . man is represented as emerging from a rude savage state, through the influence of religion. He is next personified as a hunter, and a tiller of the earth. . . . Patriarchal simplicity then becomes invaded and the worship of the true God defiled. Paganism prevails and becomes diffused by means of the Arts. The worship of the heavenly bodies . . . led the Egyptians, Chaldeans and other nations to study Astronomy, typified by the centre statues, the keystone of the composition. Civilization is now presumed to have made considerable progress. Descending towards the Western angle of the pediment, is Mathematics . . . The Drama, Poetry and Music balance the group of the Fine Arts on the Eastern side, the whole composition terminating with Natural History.

This sculptural programme was one of Westmacott's last works. Unlike his earlier designs, it indulged in a touch of polychromy: the tympanum was tinted blue and the ornaments gilded.

In this way, by the addition of sculpture and colouring Smirke's chaste composition of the 1820s moved tentatively towards those twin determinants of mid-Victorian design: plasticity and polychromy. But economy prevented the completion of this process. The grand design was never finished. Worse still, the great colonnade has never been seen to full advantage. Nash's unfinished schemes for the Trafalgar Square area (1825) had included an avenue linking Charing Cross to Bloomsbury, a tremendous vista aligned on the axis of the British Museum. And ever since Nash's project was abandoned, the re-opening of that vista has preoccupied almost every town planner who has turned his thoughts to London's north-west sector.

Working drawings for the east wing of the new museum were available in 1823, for part of the west wing in 1826, for the north wing in 1831-3 and for the southern entrance front in 1841-4. Between 1823 and 1852 the vast quadrangular structure slowly enveloped first the garden to the north of the old museum, and then the site and forecourt of the old building itself. 'And strange it was to see', wrote John Timbs, 'the lofty pitched roof, balustraded attic and large-windowed front of "the French manner" giving way to the Grecian architecture of Sir Robert Smirke's new design.' It was not until June 1847 that the 'decayed and dangerous' clock turret of Montagu House was finally removed. Altogether, it was a painfully slow process – nearly one third of a century from conception to completion. Thousands of visitors, a whole generation of scholars, came to know the clang of hammer and chisel, the whistling of labourers, and the rumble of the mortar mill. 'The building', the *Athenaeum* noted tartly in 1843, 'progresses like the Sinking Fund, by fits . . . [but] no doubt our great Doric architect builds, as Zeuxis painted, for posterity.' The *Foreign Quarterly Review* could hardly resist pointing out that public buildings went up rather more quickly in Munich. But it was the *Mechanics' Magazine* which placed the blame where it properly belonged: 'the delay in the building which has so often been attributed to [Smirke's] inaction and inattention proceeds, in reality, from the parsimony of Government, who have seldom granted more to the annual building-fund of the Museum than half what was applied for.'

The east wing was finished within five years, at a cost of £130,000. On the ground floor the King's Library, above it the Natural History collection; at the southern end manuscript rooms, and at the northern end an entrance from Montague Place and a substantial single-return staircase to the first floor. But this arrangement of the contents of the new wing was not finally established until its construction was nearly complete. The paintings which were to have occupied five rooms on the first floor – from the collections of Sir Julius Angerstein and 'that giant of amateurs', Sir George Beaumont – became instead the nucleus of the National Gallery. And Wilkins's new building in Trafalgar Square eventually incorporated those very columns from Carlton House which – in the opinion of at least one architect, P. F. Robinson – might have formed the perfect entrance to an entirely separate library building vaguely reminiscent of the Maison Carée at Nimes [57].

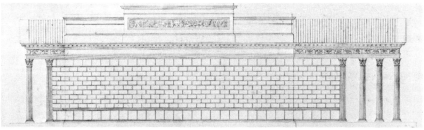

57. Design for a separate Royal Library, incorporating columns from Carlton House (1827), P. F. Robinson

But by 1829 all was settled. During the summer of that year, a fleet of vans transported the precious cargo of royal books from Kensington Palace to their new home in Bloomsbury.

Resplendent with glazed bookcases, oak flooring inlaid with mahogany, and galleries of burnished brass, the King's Library [58] was described by the *Gentleman's Magazine* as 'the encadrement of one of the most precious jewels ever attached to the Crown of England'. It was certainly a setting worthy of a collection once housed in Sir William Chambers's octagonal library at Buckingham House and nearly placed in Inigo Jones's Banqueting House in Whitehall. Consisting of a single apartment one hundred yards long, 41 feet wide and 30 feet high, with a central section 58 feet wide, the King's Library is certainly Smirke's finest interior design. In fact, it is one of the noblest rooms in London. Yet its spatial rhythms are undeniably sluggish. And the general effect of its decoration – Grecian details modified in the manner of George Dance Jr – is one of ponderous grandeur. The introduction of circular panels into the mass of plaster coffering is stylistically anomalous; and the abrupt horizontal divisions created by the galleries detract from the room's lofty effect. Eight extra columns were to have demarcated the central area. This arrangement would certainly have been impressive. But the cost of polishing each column – monoliths of Aberdeen granite with capitals of Derbyshire alabaster – turned out to be prohibitive. Only four were installed: they were bought ready-worked for £60, but the expense of polishing raised their total cost to £2,400. As a result, the yellow scagliola pilasters which delimit the central space seem insufficiently substantial – unlike the doors at either end of the room, powerfully framed with architrave and console. Stylistically hybrid and spatially dull, the King's Library is fully redeemed by the integrity and magnificence of its decoration. In particular, the details of the entablature show Smirke at his most fastidious. Alone among his works the King's Library proved almost immune to criticism.

While rooms at the southern end of the east wing – now the middle and south Manuscript Rooms – were being fitted up as reading rooms for manuscripts and printed books, work was progressing on the west wing. This block was needed primarily to re-house the Elgin Marbles. By 1825 their accommodation was said to be in a state of 'impending ruin'. And four years previously Smirke had warned the Treasury that the temporary Elgin Room [59] was highly combustible: in case of fire

58. The King's Library, Sir Robert Smirke

59. The temporary Elgin Room, Sir Robert Smirke

the marbles 'would inevitably be reduced to lime, as their weight would
preclude the possibility of removing them on any such sudden emer-
gency'. But the Tory government seemed disinclined to hurry. By 1830
only the shell had been constructed. Under the new Whig government
of that year the Treasury proved more liberal and authorized the transference of the marbles and their 'fixing . . . in the manner proposed by Mr
Westmacott'. As originally planned in 1826 the new Elgin Room was to
have projected westward at right angles to the west wing, instead of
running parallel to it. Such an east–west axis might well have supplied a
steadier light for viewing sculpture. But Westmacott was quite happy
with the eventual north–south alignment. He thought the new Elgin
Room [60] 'one of the finest rooms in the world; and . . . as finely lighted
as any room I know'.

By 1831, therefore, both floors of the east wing had been completed,
as had the new Elgin Room. Of the west wing, continuing Saunders's

60. The Elgin Room, Sir Robert Smirke

61. The Phigaleian Room. Detail of Smirke's polychrome decoration

block northwards and joining the new Elgin Room by means of the Phigaleian – later Nereid Room [61] – only the interior of the upper floor remained incomplete. Two sides of the great quadrangle, faced with Portland stone, with a single row of windows, and attached Ionic porticoes, confronted each other across the gardens of Montagu House, shaming its old colonnade which had 'long been observed to be in a deplorable state'.

In 1832 the Office of Works was reorganized – largely as a result of Nash's shifty activities at Buckingham Palace. It was united to the Department of Woods, Forests and Land Revenues and became known as the Office of Woods and Works. The three Attached Architects were displaced, and commissions were thrown open to the profession. This reorganization in no way diminished Smirke's position as architect of

62. The King's Library, Sir Robert Smirke

the British Museum. In fact he profited from the new arrangements. Besides receiving a compensatory knighthood he retained responsibility for the museum, but as an independent architect, with commission increased from 3 per cent to 5 per cent.

The cost of running repairs at Montagu House, which between 1821 and 1833 cost over £15,000, annually emphasized the necessity for further rebuilding, and in the latter year work began on the third side of the quadrangle, the north wing of the new museum. The estimate was £70,000. Within five years two new reading rooms (later the Music and Catalogue Rooms) were opened at its eastern end, with a separate entrance from Montague Place. Printed Books and Manuscripts were now distributed at either end of the King's Library [62]. But the large room in the centre of the north wing – rebuilt as the North Library,

1936–8 – was still unfinished in 1838. In that year, the number of visitors, 'increasing beyond precedent or expectation', prompted the Trustees to press the Treasury for extra grants. A Parliamentary committee, headed by Sir Robert Peel, promptly began an investigation of all accounts.

In his evidence before the committee Smirke estimated that the structural parts of his great scheme might be finished in six years at a cost of £250,000. But he added an inevitable caveat: 'should the progress of the buildings be continued in the same slow and uncertain manner as it hath hitherto been (having to the present time occupied a period of fourteen years since the commencement), I cannot give any assurance that my estimates will . . . be found correct.' In fact it was almost impossible for an architect to present global estimates for such a large building executed over so long a period of time. What Smirke did was to produce interim estimates for each section as required. As a precaution against overspending, annual Treasury grants were generally prefaced with demands for 'the utmost retrenchment' or 'the most rigid and severe economy'. But between 1823 and 1849 expenditure totalled £696,995. And by the time the new museum had been completed, in 1852, the total had soared to about £800,000. Even as the building neared completion schemes were in preparation for the circular reading room, which was to add another £150,000 to this sum. Between 1823 and 1860, when the Office of Works handed back responsibility for the structure to the Trustees, £1,090,274 13s. 6d. had been spent on rebuilding, £113,367 on repairs and £44,924 on the purchase of land – in all, more than one and a quarter million pounds.

The decade 1839–49 was occupied by the construction of the Arch Room (1840–41, for storing the library's incunabula) [63]; the Lycian Gallery (1845, later the Archaic Greek Sculpture Gallery and now the Early Greek Room); the Phigaleian Gallery (1847, now the Payava Room); the Long Room parallel to the King's Library (1846–50, for book storage); and the great southern entrance façade (1841–8). As the entrance front grew, so old Montagu House was progressively demol-

63. The Arch Room (1841), Sir Robert Smirke

ished, in three stages. Sites for two blocks of Keepers' houses were prepared on either side of a new forecourt, partly on land freshly purchased from the Duke of Bedford. During this period of transition the Principal Librarian, Sir Henry Ellis, resided at 70 Great Russell Street, specially fitted up for the purpose. Between 1844 and 1849 the Keepers' houses were constructed, first the western block and then the eastern.

Eighteen forty was a crucial year in the architectural history of the museum. In that year a deputation headed by Sir Robert Peel persuaded the Treasury to sanction a higher rate of expenditure, and plans were at last put in hand for the construction of the entrance façade. Messrs Grissell and Peto who had submitted the lowest tender for the south front, began work in September 1841, but in the following July transfered their contract to Messrs Baker and Sons, the builders of the other three wings and contractors for the majority of Smirke's London works. Smirke's sister Sarah had married the head of the firm, Samuel Baker of Rochester, and this special relationship between architect and builder did not escape the notice of Smirke's more malicious critics. The architect's specification stipulated 'hard, sound, grey stock bricks . . . mortar of Dorking, Halling or other stone lime . . . ground to a fine powder and mixed . . . with clean sand taken from the river [Thames] above Blackfriars' Bridge'; iron cramps for the stonework of Portland and Yorkshire stone; 'best best Memel, Riga and Danzig timber; Cragleith and Gazeby stone for the steps and paving of the portico, and for the main staircase, 'steps and landings of stone from Elland Edge or other of the hardest and most compact quality of Yorkshire stone'. By 1842 the walls had reached roof level, and Messrs Kepp were employed to cover the roof with copper. No competition was held for this particular contract. 'The material is so rarely used', Smirke informed the Commissioners of Woods and Works, 'that I do not know of any other tradesmen employed in such work except upon a very small scale.' Messrs Robson and Estall were chosen as plasterers: 'all the ceilings are to be lathed with double laths made of sound fir, nailed with nails of wrought or cast iron

. . . with Keene's cement for the plastering of the walls of the principal rooms.' Messrs Collman and Davis were responsible for interior decoration. Glazing was supplied by Messrs Cobbett & Son. All these tradesmen were customary Office of Works contractors.

The entrance front, indeed the whole museum, gave Smirke a chance to display both the Grecian style and his mastery of constructional techniques upon the largest possible scale. The spacious, box-like galleries, his whole conception of a modernized Grecian architecture, rational, austere and economical, depended upon concrete and cast iron. At Millbank Penitentiary on the banks of the Thames, he had – in 1817 – been the first English architect to demonstrate the value of concrete foundations. Previously, marshy sites had been stabilized by means of wooden sleepers or piling. There is no evidence that concrete was used for the foundations of the King's Library in 1823 or for the first section

64. Laying the foundations of the Lycian Gallery (1845). George Scharf Sr

of the west wing in 1825. The ground was presumably strong enough to support brick footings set in cement. But numerous working drawings survive to show that a concrete base between 2 feet 6 inches and 6 feet thick was used for the later wings, that is for all work after 1833 [64]. The concrete raft supporting the colonnade is in places more than 6 feet thick.

Concrete was not the only new material employed. Fireproofing was supplied in the form of slate flooring by William North and copper roofing by Messrs Kepp. Besides traditional decorative materials such as marble, mahogany and bronze, much use was made of scagliola, papier maché, Keene's Cement and encaustic polycromy by Collman and Davis in hypothetically Grecian hues. Cast iron, disguised by plaster coffering and moulded beams, supported the ceiling and roof of every room, from the joists of the prefabricated Elgin Room (1816) to the beams (Foster Rastrick & Co., Ironbridge, 1824) of the King's Library, where Smirke even considered replacing the central pillars of polished granite by exposed cast iron columns. Messrs Dewar, who contracted for most of the later ironwork, including that supporting the great entrance front, were told to use 'castings made from pigs of the best English iron . . . all perfectly sound and smooth', tested by weights in the foundry under the architect's supervision, and 'secured from rust by two coats of lithic or other oil paint'. 'Considering the very unusual size of the beams required,' added Smirke, 'I am anxious to have the castings made by founders upon whom . . . I may rely.' The cast iron beams supporting the entrance entablature were in places more than 43 feet long, and were tested to bear a weight of thirty tons. As with the rest of the building, the huge facing slabs of Portland stone were tied to a brick core with iron cramps. In 1850, soon after the completion of the colonnade, C. R. Cockerell was able to tell his Royal Academy students: 'since the days of Hadrian no such stones have been used . . . the front . . . is formed by 800 stones, each from 5 to 9 tons in weight. Even St Paul's contains no approach to these magnitudes.'

It was the King's Library which set structural standards for the whole museum. The room's unusual length (300 feet) required brickwork of unusual strength and thickness. Its unusual width (41 feet overall; 58 feet in the centre) required cast iron beams of exceptional span. Commenting on the 'massy' nature of the walls, C. W. Pasley – an expert on structural techniques – noticed that they were from 5½ to 6 bricks thick, built with mortar composed of one part Dorking lime to only three parts Thames sand, grouted externally with liquefied cement and surrounded by a false area as a precaution against damp. Smirke's use of cast iron in the ceiling of the King's Library constituted something of a revolution in metropolitan architecture. Much of the credit belongs to John Rastrick (1780–1856), one of the period's leading railway engineers. In 1810 Smirke had used built-in cast iron bearers over 30 feet in length at Earl Bathurst's house, Cirencester Park. This was perhaps the first large-scale use of cast iron beams in English domestic architecture. But thirteen years later, in 1823, Smirke hestitated to span the width of the King's Library with beams cast in one section more than 40 feet long. Instead he proposed to make use of a trussed girder composed of sections of cast and wrought iron. Two years previously Rastrick had laid a report before Parliament on the cast iron beams, 35–6 feet long, used by Nash at Buckingham Palace. He now assured Smirke that in 1821 he had personally directed the use of beams no less than 90 feet long for the Stourport Bridge over the river Severn. Rastrick's beams for the King's Library had a flanged section and mostly measured 41 feet long. Some were more than 50 feet in length. Their depth varied according to an elliptical curve from 3 feet at mid-span to 1 foot 9 inches near the ends, finishing with a quadrant. The ceilings were of arched iron plates, an eighth of an inch thick, stiffened by light angle irons, carried on the bottom flanges of the beams. Rastrick later informed a Parliamentary committee that they were 'the first beams that were ever introduced into London of so great a length and with large openings through the web of the beam'. They were tested in 1824 with a dead weight of 40 tons. All in all, it was a triumphant example of the use of this new material in a major public building. But Rastrick complained that he made no profit on this important contract because of the rising cost of pig iron.

When the Egyptian rooms were being altered in the early 1930s, several girders were removed and subjected to rigorous investigation. As might have been expected, the results showed that Smirke and Rastrick had been ingenious rather than scientific. By perforating the web of the girders with long oval voids they reduced their weight and made handling easier. At the same time, these 'Vierendeel' perforations set up secondary stresses, and effectively converted a deep girder into two shallow beams, each susceptible to lateral buckling. The thickness of the flange thus became quite inadequate, and the whole girder was therefore at least partly dependent on the lateral support of secondary wooden beams. Still, there was nothing unusual in that. Most of the girders employed in early nineteenth-century building were similarly used in conjunction with wooden beams, or else were built in with brick jack-arches, the thrust of which was taken by iron tie-rods.

One other novelty was incorporated into the structure of the new museum: central heating. During the 1820s and 1830s several new systems of heating and ventilation were developed in Britain. With cisterns, furnaces and cumbrous pipes, they were crude in principle and uncertain in effect. Smirke was something of a pioneer in their adoption: C. J. Richardson's *Warming and Ventilation* (1837) was dedicated to him. He used Price and Manby's system in the Elgin and Egyptian Galleries, and Stratton and Oldham's system at the General Post Office. He used Perkins's system in the Museum Print Room, Bird Room and reading rooms; in the Custom House Long Room; in his own office at 5, Stratford Place, near Oxford Street; and in the temporary Houses of Parliament, built to accommodate Commons and Lords while Barry and Pugin's great work was slowly completed. In 1836 a Parliamentary committee was told how well the British Museum's central heating was operating: Bloomsbury readers seldom shivered, unlike scholars in the Royal Library at Paris, who 'must keep themselves warm as well as they can'. Two years later *The Times* praised not only the function of the reading rooms' heaters but also their appearance: four 'great sort of chests of hot water pipes' covered with marble slabs to appear 'exceedingly classical and ornamental'. But in the long run Smirke's heating of the British Museum can hardly be called successful. The 'Museum Headache' and 'Museum Megrims', like the Long Room Fever at the Custom House, and perhaps even the unfortunate death of Mr Smith, Curator of the Print Room, were all signs of the inadequacy of these ephemeral patent processes.

As his greatest commission, under his immediate supervision for over twenty years, the British Museum made considerable demands on Smirke's professional ability, particularly during the closing stages of his career. After 1842 he was frequently unwell and occupied an office in the remaining portion of Montagu House in order to direct the work more effectively. As the great colonnade rose higher, the museum alone retained his personal attention, other commissions being delegated to his younger brother, Sydney Smirke (1799-1877). But within four months of his father's death in May 1845, ill health forced Smirke himself to take a holiday in Nice. In the following year he retired from practice altogether. That left Sydney Smirke responsible for all the unfinished sections of the museum. These were chiefly the forecourt and lodges (1849-53); the Ephesus Room (1850-51, now the Room of the Harpy Tomb) connecting the Elgin and Lycian Rooms and first assigned to Greek sculpture; the narrow galleries (1851, now Nimrud and Nineveh Galleries) first designed for Assyrian sculpture, parallel to the Egyptian Galleries; the first and second Graeco-Roman Rooms (1852-3, now the Cycladic Room); the Assyrian Saloon (1856, now the Assyrian Gallery) between, and parallel to, the existing Greek and Assyrian Galleries; and the northern extension of the Elgin Room (1868, now the Room of the Caryatid). Sydney Smirke's son, Sydney Smirke Jr (1838-1912), who

65. Sydney Smirke's railings, Sir Robert Smirke's portico
and Sir Richard Westmacott's sculpture 'The Progress of Civilization'

designed the lion's head water-basin in the portico, was the last of the family to be associated with the museum.

The fine railings at the entrance [65], cast at York by John Walker & Co., were also designed by Sydney Smirke. He intended the massive granite gatepiers to act as plinths for decorative sculpture by Westmacott. Bacon, Newton, Milton and Shakespeare were the luminaries suggested. Unfortunately these sculptures – like those planned for the great staircase in the entrance hall [66] – were never installed. Rather less unfortunate was the abandonment of another idea – solid granite walls twelve feet high, on either side of the central railings, designed to screen the keepers' houses from the eyes of curious pedestrians. An announcement in the House of Commons that this barricade would cost £24,100 proved 'a pleasantry beyond the digestion of members. . . . Think of walling up the work of a quarter of a century and the representative of a sum that would buy a small kingdom, in order that some officer of the establishment might not be looked in on at his dinner!' Alternative suggestions were the use of Nash's Doric colonnade from the Regent Street Quadrant, or the use of railings from St Paul's Cathedral. But in the end Sydney Smirke's railings were installed, resplendent and uncluttered. Their gilding alone cost £385.

Until 1896 the entrance lodges were guarded on the Great Russell Street side by a quaint anachronism: a low railing which marked the boundary of the museum and at the same time prevented 'nuisances' in the days before public lavatories. Four of the little bronze lions which once embellished this curious survival, now decorate the marble chimneypieces of the Trustees' Boardroom. Others surround the Wellington monument in St Paul's Cathedral. They were modelled by no less an artist than Alfred Stevens (1818–75), working from Sydney Smirke's drawing of the lion at the foot of the staircase of the Bargello in Florence. Stevens's 'cat', as he used to call it, became one of the most popular decorative symbols in late Victorian Britain. Copies can still be seen *inter alia* on railings outside Ely House and the Law Society in London, and outside the City Museum, Leicester.

Sir Robert Smirke's reputation suffered greatly from the museum's slow construction. Had his original design been published in 1823 it would probably have been hailed as a masterpiece. Instead, its completion was widely regarded as a disaster. Conceived as the choicest product of the English Greek Revival, the British Museum was finished, amid mounting hostility, a generation too late. When the new Elgin Room was unveiled in 1831, it was greeted with loud applause. One critic was thrown into 'mental ecstasy' by this 'beautiful and brilliant' design: 'our first view . . . was a moment of . . . overpowering emotion. . . . We felt on classic ground! . . . Honour to Smirke!' By the 1840s, however, Regency 'chastity' seemed too meagre, too tame, to be tolerated by a new generation of Victorian critics. So Smirke's last efforts were greeted with abuse, and for a long time his memory was treated with condescension. It was a sad end to his career.

Criticism was mounted on three fronts: planning, style and patronage. As regards planning, Smirke's museum was open to several objections. The layout of the galleries was formal rather than convenient, and practical rather than scientific. Function had been sacrificed to grandeur in the shape of courtyard and colonnade. The lighting of both the north and west wings was impeded by 'a wretched pseudo-portico of three quarter columns' – the vestigial relic of Smirke's original quadrangular scheme. The Roman Gallery, which apart from the Lycian Room was alone aligned on that east-west axis which provided the most suitable light, was shaded by the colonnade. The finest situation for any sculpture gallery was occupied by the main staircase. And then there was the anomaly of the empty quadrangle. James Fergusson, an early and articulate apostle of functionalism, published a damning catalogue of errors. But that was in 1849, twenty-six years after the museum was planned. Judged by Regency standards, Smirke's original plan struck a fair balance between convenience and beauty. It was the explosive expansion of

66. The Great Staircase, Sir Robert Smirke

the museum, not the inadequacy of Smirke's layout, which turned Britain's Temple of the Arts into a museologist's nightmare.

As regards patronage, there was some justice in the claim that Smirke owed his appointment as architect to an outworn and monopolistic system. By the 1840s, the principle of architectural competition was widely accepted: it was not until the 1860s that the mismanagement of competitions undermined public confidence in free-market aesthetics. Meanwhile, Smirke was abused as a Tory stooge, appointed during Lord Liverpool's government and maintained during Sir Robert Peel's. 'Has so little advance been made by the people in architectural taste', asked the *Athenaeum*, 'that what would have passed . . . in 1823, will now satisfy them in 1844? . . . The principle of publicity having been adopted . . . in the instance of the New Houses of Parliament, ought . . . to be adopted in all similar circumstances.' There was no denying that Smirke had taken office in 1815 as a Tory nominee. A decade of Whig government during the 1830s had left his position unimpaired, and Sir Robert Peel had remained a staunch supporter although in Opposition. Now Smirke was paying the penalty for his political allegiance. Peel returned to power in 1841, the year in which work began on the great colonnade, and the fury of his opponents is reflected in the bitterness of their criticism. As Conservative papers *The Times* remained silent and the *Builder* prevaricated. Other periodicals were less inhibited. Most violent of all was the *Civil Engineer and Architect's Journal*:

> What if a 'morning star', as Pugin calls it, be rising at Westminster, all is Cimmerian darkness at Bloomsbury, where Smirkean night – or knight-hood – is suffered to reign supreme. . . . All . . . stand in awe of the prime minister and his pet. . . . It is impossible for any one to say of Sir Robert Smirke that he is a temporizing or time-serving man, since instead of at all bending to the spirit of the present time . . . he shows himself a staunch conservative in maintaining that system of monopoly and irresponsibility under which he has flourished. The public is to him the same ignoramus, insignificant public as it was some thirty years ago . . . [The museum will be] doubly *Bobbified*. . . . Sir Robert Peel may be a very good *Cabinet*-maker, Sir Robert Smirke an excellent warehouse-builder,

but let them stick to those trades, and not foist upon the country such a dowdy design as the one concocted for the British Museum out of the Post Office and the Custom House. . . . Something more than Sir Robert's formal stereotype Ionic is here required.

More simply, the *Spectator* merely called on the museum's architect to 'resign and abdicate'.

As regards style, much of the criticism Smirke received reflects no more than a shift in taste, from Regency to Victorian. The abler critics admitted that, within the context of Greek Revival theory, Smirke's design could hardly be bettered. Ruskin recognized its essential nobility. And even Fergusson had to admit that neither 'the Berlin Museum, nor the Munich [Regensburg] Walhalla, or Glyptothek, nor the Paris Madeleine, or Bourse . . ., considering the difficulties of the subject, . . . show more taste or knowledge of the style.' It was the lesser critics, the run-of-the-mill press pundits, who attacked the museum most fiercely. Abuse was showered upon the 'formalised deformity, shrivelled precision, and starved accuracy' of this 'miserable abortion'. Having 'lived over the period for which he was so well adapted and run into another', the idol of the Regency – Britain's 'classic genius' – became a whipping boy for Victorian aesthetes. 'Poor Smirke!', trumpeted one journal,

how greatly he is to be pitied!, and for the very reason that many now envy him, to wit, because he has had so many opportunities of manifesting his imbecility. Barry—Smirke, they are as far asunder as two poles. . . . Mr Barry's ideas are so *elastic* – he has such a superabundance of imagination and invention that we wish he would out of charity's sake bestow a little of it, some of the mere crumbs and sweepings, upon Sir Robert Smirke, they would surely be acceptable to an architectural Lazarus.

There was some truth in the joke that the forecourt wings – 'commonplace' and 'cockney' – made the portico look like 'Miltiades between two City "gents".' But the craving for ornament induced by Pugin's Gothic and Barry's palazzos produced such absurdities as: 'Smirke has contrived to make his Ionic colonnades look no better than mere *frippery*, a sort of architectural "cover-slut" to a very ugly and mean-looking brick building.'

In fact – inside and out – the British Museum is a magnificent essay in the adaptation and integration of antique sources. Besides the Temple of Athena Polias at Priene and the Temple of Dionysus at Teos, there are hints of the Erechtheion, the Ilissus Temple, the Theseion, the Thrasyllus monument, and the Propylaea. Until the construction of the new Houses of Parliament it was the largest secular building in London. Its completion fully merited the award of the R.I.B.A. Gold Medal in 1853. The mouldings which adorn the façades of the entrance front and quadrangle are impeccably finished, and the side-lit or top-lit galleries, articulated by Doric columns and antae and diversified only by the cool polychromy of their beamed and coffered ceilings, form a splendid, if insufficiently anonymous, backcloth for the display of antiquities. The solemn counterpoint of portico, wings and enveloping colonnade, massive stylobate and inflected parapet, extorted even from the giddiest critics a grudging recognition of the composition's kinetic power. Smirke's serene design fused the Grecian combination of surface modelling and complementary planes with the spatial dynamics of Palladian tradition. In Covent Garden Theatre and the British Museum he gave London the first and last of its great buildings in the Grecian style. His monumental creation in a Bloomsbury backstreet constituted the high water mark of the English Greek Revival, and furnished the movement with a ponderous *finale*.

5 : The Round Reading Room

'Paris must be surpassed!' (Thomas Watts, 1837)

The first British Museum reading room was in the 'base storey' at the west corner of Montagu House. It was dimly lit by only two windows which rattled in the wind; the floor consisted of bare boards covered with rush matting; the walls were lined with stuffed birds; and in the middle stood one baize-covered table surrounded by twenty chairs. But it was enough. There were very few readers, and they could escape from these cramped quarters if they wished, through a conveniently glazed door into the aromatic gardens maintained by the officers of the botanical section. Among the first eight readers who arrived on the very first day was that apostle of the Greek Revival, 'Athenian' Stuart. Six months later the poet Gray arrived and wrote off some impressions to his friend Mason:

I am just settled in my new habitation in Southampton Row. . . . The Museum will be my chief amusement. I this day passed through the jaws of a great leviathon [a whale in the Department of Natural and Artificial Productions] . . . into the belly of Dr Templeman, Superintendent of the Reading Room, who congratulated himself on the sight of so much good company. We were – a man that writes for Lord Royston; a man that writes for Dr Barton of York; a third that writes for the Emperor of Germany or Dr Peacock, for he speaks the worst English I ever heard; Dr Stukeley who writes for himself, the very worst person he could write for; and I, who only read to know if there were anything worth writing, and that not without some difficulty. I find that they printed one thousand copies of the Harleian Catalogue, and sold four-score; that they have £900 p.a. income and spend £1300, and that they are building apartments for the under-keepers; so I expect . . . to see the collection advertised and set to auction.

But a month later the reading room was still open and Gray was happy to 'pass four hours in the day' there, the 'stillness and solitude' broken only by 'Dr Stukeley the antiquary, who comes there to talk nonsense and coffee-house news'.

Such were the early days of Britain's national library. Readers remained a select company till the end of the eighteenth century. Dr Johnson was admitted in 1761; Gibbon followed in 1770; and Boswell arrived in 1778. As the *Synopsis* of 1808 put it, the reading room was only available to 'men of letters and artists . . . not wholly strangers. . . . Strangers are not conducted through [the library] as the mere sight of the outside of books cannot convey either instruction or amusement'. Benjamin Disraeli recalled that 'when my father first frequented the reading room . . . at the end of the last century, his companions never numbered half a dozen'. 'There we were,' wrote Isaac D'Israeli, 'little attended to, musing in silence and oblivion; for sometimes we had to wait a day or two till the volumes so eagerly demanded, slowly appeared.' Ladies were generally only admitted in pairs.

In 1774 the reading room made its first move, upstairs. Two rooms in the north-west corner of Montagu House were thrown into one. And so began that process of absorbing extra rooms which was repeated in 1803, 1809, 1817 and 1823. The number of readers had begun to grow. During the French Revolutionary period in particular, numbers were swollen by clerical emigrés: the reading room had already begun its career as a haunt of political exiles. As they became more popular, these small rooms in Montagu House became slightly more efficient, with catalogues and reference books on the shelves and a system of ordering books by tugging a bell-rope. These were the rooms which Washington Irving discovered in 1815 and happily described in Geoffrey Crayon's *Sketchbook* (1820). Sauntering one day in the museum, and tiring of Egyptian mummies, his attention strayed to a distant door:

It was closed, but every now and then it would open, and some strange favoured being, generally clothed in black, would steal forth, and glide through the rooms, without noticing any of the surrounding objects. There was an air of mystery about this that piqued my languid curiosity, and I determined to . . . explore [these] unknown regions . . . The door yielded to my hand, with all that facility with which the portals of enchanted castles yield to the adventurous knight-errant. I found myself in a spacious chamber, surrounded with great cases of venerable books. Above the cases, and just under the cornice, were arranged a great number of quaint black-looking portraits of ancient authors. About the room were placed long tables, with stands for reading and writing, at which sat many pale, cadaverous personages, poring intently over dusty volumes, rummaging among mouldy manuscripts, and taking copious notes of their contents. The most hushed stillness reigned throughout this mysterious apartment, excepting that you might hear the racing of pens over sheets of paper, or occasionally the deep sigh of one of these sages, as he shifted his position to turn over the page of an old folio; doubtless arising from that hollowness and flatulency incident to learned research. Now and then one of these personages would write something on a small slip of paper, and ring a bell, whereupon a familiar would appear, take the paper in profound silence, glide out of the room, and return shortly after loaded with ponderous tomes, upon which the other would fall tooth and nail with famished voracity. I had no longer a doubt that I had happened upon a body of magi, deeply engaged in the study of occult sciences. . . . My curiosity being now fully aroused, I whispered to one of the familiars, as he was about to leave the room, and begged an interpretation of the strange scene before me. A few words were sufficient for the purpose. I found that these mysterious personages, whom I had mistaken for magi, were principally authors, and in the very act of manufacturing books. I was, in fact, in the reading room of the great British Library.

But having penetrated the inner sanctum, our intruder promptly succumbed to the drowsy atmosphere and fell asleep on a pile of old folios. Dreaming that the portraits on the walls came to life and descended in rage upon the plagiarists below, he burst out laughing – 'a sound never before heard in that grave sanctuary' – and awoke, to find himself evicted for entering the reading room without a ticket.

The quaint world of Geoffrey Crayon passed away in 1829 when the reading room moved again, out of Montagu House and into part of Sir Robert Smirke's new east wing. Readers were transferred to two rooms

to the south of the King's Library, now the middle and south manuscript
rooms but then 'approached by a labyrinth, leading along a gutter and
over two drains'. There they stayed until 1838 when Smirke's north
wing was at last ready to receive them. In that year two new reading
rooms were established, a large one for printed books and a small one for
manuscripts. These tall apartments [67], later subdivided as the Music

67. The old reading room, Sir Robert Smirke

and Catalogue Rooms, accommodated twenty-six tables with eight seats
each – nearly twice as many places as before. Ten thousand reference
books were placed close to hand. The chair legs, noted the *Quarterly
Review*, were 'padded with india-rubber to move noiselessly like cats
paws'. Books arrived in minutes as if 'by magic'. Yet the number of
readers – and the number of books – continued to expand alarmingly.
Despite – or perhaps because of – Smirke's central heating, the crowded

rooms became foetid and unwholesome. Mrs Lynn-Linton remembered them as 'badly-lighted, ill-ventilated and queerly tenanted'. George Augustus Sala thought them 'spacious, but rather musty-smelling'. Blotting paper had replaced sand, but museum 'megrims' were still a frequent affliction, and Carlyle complained loudly of 'reading-room headache'. 'The ordinary frequenters', he lamented, 'are a very thick-skinned race – I am a thin-skinned student and can't study there.' In fact, as the 1840s progressed, these reading rooms became something of a public joke. 'Every class of persons haunts the place', complained *Bentley's Miscellany* in 1852, 'from the literary lawyer's clerk to the revolutionary notorieties of Europe. There are hebdomadal humorists purloining jokes, third-rate dramatists plundering plots, girls copying heads and flowers . . .' But *The Times* was wildly exaggerating when it complained, in 1854:

In this delectable chamber are generally to be found three to four hundred persons of all descriptions, among whom the shabby genteel greatly preponderate. Some fifty or sixty of these are employed in making extracts from encyclopaedias and books of reference; some two hundred and fifty are reading novels and the remainder are employed in looking at prints. Among the crowd are generally to be found a lunatic or two, sent there by his relatives to keep him out of mischief.

In fact, during the 1840s, the collections of printed books and manuscripts at the British Museum had already begun to emerge as one of the great libraries of the world. This development was almost entirely due to the ruthless energy of one man, the man who became Keeper of Printed Books in 1837, and sixth Principal Librarian in 1856, Sir Anthony Panizzi (1797–1879), the 'Napoleon of Librarians' [68]. The title 'Principal Librarian' had originally no special connection with the Department of Printed Books – all the original Keepers were known as Under Librarians. Not until long after Panizzi's death was the title belatedly changed to 'Director and Principal Librarian'. The fact that the new title was not

68. *Sir Anthony Panizzi* (1797–1879).
From a cartoon by Ape (C. Pellegrini), 1874

simply, and more logically, 'Director', is perhaps an oblique testimony to Panizzi's posthumous influence. Thanks to his efforts, the future of the museum as an institution became intimately tied up with the functions of the library.

The first three Principal Librarians, all medical men, were hardly fully employed at the museum. Dr Gowin Knight, 1756-72, eked out his income by selling venetian blinds and magnetic compasses; Dr Matthew Paty, 1772-6, combined his office with the secretaryship of the Royal Society; and Dr Charles Morton 1776-99, enjoyed several subsidiary sources of revenue. After all, their salary was only £200 per annum, and the British Museum had yet to assume its later status as a major national institution. Joseph Planta's tenure of office, 1799-1827, marked a turning point – though he too was a pluralist, being Paymaster of Exchequer Bills. He saw the number of readers increase from less than two hundred to more than six hundred a year, the number of artists from less than twenty to nearly three hundred, and the number of visitors from less than 12,000 to nearly 130,000. And he initiated what soon became one of the museum's most valuable functions, the publication of lists and catalogues. But his successor, Sir Henry Ellis, 1827-56, was hardly the man to maintain this momentum. A genial, conservative scholar, he was ill-suited to face the crisis of the 1820s and 1830s. Like his predecessors, he lived to a great age: Morton died at 83, Planta at 84 and Ellis at 92 – Baber, Panizzi's predecessor as Keeper of Printed Books, lived to the age of 94. These were calm and peaceful days for the officers who lived in the crumbling courtyard of Montagu House. Back in 1765 Miss Catherine Talbot had envied them their 'comfortable apartments in the wings', and their 'philosophic grove and physic garden open to the view of a delightful country'. Of course there was gossip and there were quarrels. In the 1760s Gray remarked that they fought like Fellows of an Oxford college. And in 1768 the Trustees had to remind all officers to behave 'like gentlemen living under the same roof'. But for a man like Ellis, the British Museum was a haven of peace. For Panizzi it was a battleground.

Like Paty and Planta, Panizzi was a foreigner, a hero of the Italian *risorgimento*. But he identified himself completely with the reformation and expansion of the museum, particularly the department of Printed Books. During the eighteenth century, natural history had been the museum's strongest section; during the Regency antiquities. Now it was the library's turn. Cometh the hour, cometh the man. Panizzi's subordinates came to dread his 'arrogance . . . irritability . . . and . . . notorious verbosity'. Sir Edmund Gosse remembered him as 'a thorough-going tyrant'. Sir Percy Gardner likened his impact to that of 'a steam-roller'. Arundell Esdaile compares his presence in the British Museum to 'an Italian volcano in a Dutch garden', but adds: 'as a library administrator he has never had a rival; he throws Bignon, Korf and Delisle into the shade.' Under Panizzi's belligerent direction, the library came to dominate the museum during the Victorian period. Its expansion was certainly phenomenal. In 1759 there were about 50,000 printed volumes; in 1800, 65,000; in 1823, 125,000. On 25 July 1838, during the transference of the library from Montagu House to Smirke's north wing, the whole collection was counted for the first time and found to contain 235,000 volumes. When it was counted again on 15 December 1849, the number had grown to 435,000. By 1851, the year of the Great Exhibition, the total had risen to half a million. Between 1836 and 1851 the number of books increased at the rate of 16,000 volumes a year.

Ellis presided nominally over this expansion. When he became Principal Librarian there were less than 150,000 printed books; when he retired there were more than 520,000. But the motive power came from Panizzi. His appointment as Keeper of Printed Books in the year of Victoria's accession marked a watershed in the museum's history – he defeated a representative of the old order, shy Henry Cary, translator of Dante. And before long he built up a remarkable team of assistants – three, in particular: Thomas Watts (1811–69), a self-taught polymath of enormous energy; Edward Edwards (1812–86), a pioneer of the public library system; and the quietly industrious John Winter Jones (1805–81),

Panizzi's eventual successor. From the start Panizzi was determined on two things: to make the library the finest in the world; and, if necessary, to make the requisite space available by removing the natural history sections to a separate site. His 'great object', wrote Macaulay, 'has been to make our library the best in Europe, and [he] would at any time give three mammoths for an Aldus.' As regards the expansion of the library, Panizzi succeeded during his own lifetime. As regards the removal of natural history collections, he succeeded some twenty years after his death.

How, then, did the British Museum library compare with its British and European rivals? In 1848, with 370,000 books, it ranked only sixth among the great libraries of the world. It was surpassed by the Bibliothèque Nationale at Paris and by the royal libraries of Munich, Berlin, Petersburg and Copenhagen. Paris headed the list with 800,000 volumes. Oxford had 218,000, Cambridge 135,000, Trinity College Dublin 117,600 and Edinburgh University 96,000. By comparison, the United States Library of Congress was still in its infancy: in 1855 it still had only 60,000 volumes. Under Panizzi's direction, the British Museum began to expand faster than any of its competitors. Paris was the chief rival. During the second quarter of the nineteenth century the future Bibliothèque Nationale was struggling to absorb the immense accessions which had doubled its holdings during the Revolutionary period. The oldest of Europe's national libraries, based on the collections of medieval kings, endowed by great ministers of state like Richelieu, Mazarin and Colbert, reorganized during the eighteenth century by successive generations of the Bignon family, and now enriched by monastic spoil – the French National Library was a standing reproach to British patriotism – patriotism which a foreigner like Panizzi knew how to exploit. 'Paris', he reminded his assistants, 'must be surpassed!'

Panizzi's plan for expanding the library was threefold: larger government grants for the purchase of books; rigid enforcement of the copyright laws; and better accommodation for readers.

As long ago as 1777 Edmund Burke had asked the House of Commons to increase the annual grant made to the whole British Museum from £3,000 to £5,000. He was supported in debate by that inveterate rebel John Wilkes who, as a regular reader, complained: 'the British Museum is rich in manuscripts . . . but is wretchedly poor in printed books.' But regular Parliamentary grants continued at the same meagre level. Cobbett represented a fairly typical view when he dismissed the museum as an unnecessary drain on the public purse. Between 1801 and 1832 Printed Books received less than £20,000 of public money. And during the Parliamentary Inquiry of 1835-6 Panizzi made the reason quite clear. 'Public opinion', he stated, 'is exercised only upon one of the purposes for which the British Museum was instituted: that is, upon its establishment as a show place. Unfortunately as to its most important and most noble purpose, as an establishment for the furtherance of education, for study and research, the public seems to be almost indifferent.' He demanded a real National Library.

Panizzi laid down the programme for its formation as soon as he became Keeper of Printed Books in 1837:

First, the attention of the Keeper of this emphatically British Library ought to be directed, most particularly, to British works, and to works relating to the British Empire; its religious, political, and literary, as well as scientific history; its laws, institutions, description, commerce, arts etc. The rarer and more expensive a work of this description is, the more indefatigable efforts ought to be made to secure it . . . Secondly, the old and rare, as well as the critical, editions of ancient Classics, ought never to be sought for in vain in this Collection. Nor ought good comments, as also the best translations into modern languages, to be wanting. Thirdly, with respect to foreign literature, arts, and sciences, the Library ought to possess the best editions of standard works for critical purposes as for use. The Public have, moreover, a right to find, in their National Library, heavy as well as expensive foreign works, such as *Literary Journals*; *Transactions of Societies*; large Collections, historical or otherwise; complete series of Newspapers; Collections of Laws, and their best interpreters.

That was Panizzi's programme. Its purpose was even more inspiring than its scope. 'I want', he told a Parliamentary Committee, 'a poor student to have the same means of indulging his learned curiosity, of following his rational pursuits, of consulting the same authorities, of fathoming the most intricate inquiry, as the richest man in the kingdom, as far as books go, and I contend that government is bound to give him the most liberal and unlimited assistance in this respect.'

But what of the expense? 'The expense', concluded Panizzi in his report of 1845, 'will no doubt be great; but so is the nation which is to bear it.' The result of his pleading was a Treasury grant of £10,000, repeated each year for half a century. By 1848 the British Museum was adding 30,000 volumes per annum to its collection, as against only 12,000 in Paris, 10,000 in Munich, 5,000 in Berlin, 2,000 in Petersburg and 1,000 in Copenhagen. The figure for the next largest British library, the Bodleian, was 4,480.

These new volumes came from two chief sources: books purchased from abroad, and British books received under the copyright acts. As regards the selection and purchase of foreign publications, Panizzi was immensely helped by the indefatigable Thomas Watts. As Watts put it in 1861, he and Panizzi worked together for a quarter of a century to

bring together from all quarters the useful, the elegant, and the curious literature of every language; to unite with the best English Library in England, or the world, the best Russian Library out of Russia, the best German out of Germany, the best Spanish out of Spain, and so with every language from Italian to Icelandic, from Polish to Portuguese. In five of [these] languages . . . [the British Museum] now claims this species of supremacy, in Russian, Polish, Hungarian, Danish, and Swedish. . . . Every future student of the less-known literatures of Europe will find riches where I found poverty.

As regards books published in Britain, proper coverage demanded firm enforcement of the copyright laws. These laws stemmed initially from governmental systems of censorship in the seventeenth century.

According to the Licensing Act of 1662, copies of licensed books were to be placed in the Royal Library and in the libraries of Oxford and Cambridge. That was more than a century after the start of compulsory book deposits in the Royal Library at Paris. The Licensing Act lapsed in 1695 and was eventually replaced by the Copyright Act of 1709. According to this Act, all British publications were to be registered at Stationers' Hall in London. Nine privileged libraries had the right to claim copies of all registered works: the Royal Library; those of Oxford, Cambridge, St Andrews, Glasgow, Aberdeen and Edinburgh universities; the library of Sion College, London; and the Advocates' Library, Edinburgh. In 1801, following the Act of Union, this list was extended to include Trinity College and the King's Inns, Dublin. But during the eighteenth century few books were registered, and fewer still were claimed. And anyway, eleven privileged libraries represented an unnecessarily large threat to the finances of small but conscientious publishers. In 1836, therefore, in return for regular cash payments, the privilege was withdrawn from the four Scottish universities, Sion College and the King's Inns.

When the old Royal Library was transferred to Bloomsbury in 1757, the copyright privilege came with it. But little was done to secure enforcement until 1815 when a person was specially appointed at Stationers' Hall to receive books destined for the British Museum. Even then, the number of books involved remained small. This was the situation when Panizzi became Keeper of Printed Books. His efforts to secure tighter control were first rewarded in 1842 when the Imperial Copyright Act obliged publishers to deliver volumes *directly* to the British Museum, a privilege not enjoyed by any other library. Even so, enforcement remained lax until 1850. In that year Panizzi managed to transfer to the Department of Printed Books the Trustees' power of attorney – the power to take legal action against defaulting publishers. That did the trick. Books began to pour in. In 1851 the number of volumes received under copyright was only 9,871. By 1858 the figure was 19,578. And the number continued to grow, reinforced eventually by the New Imperial Copyright Act of 1911.

When Smirke's new museum was planned in 1823 the number of printed manuscript volumes was together less than 200,000. By 1860 the total for printed books alone was 600,000 – and it was increasing at the rate of 20,000 per annum. This trebling of a national library, unassisted by revolution or conquest, in less than a third of a century, was quite unprecedented. For every reader in 1799 there were nearly one hundred in 1835 – and that was only the beginning. The number of readers' visits rose from 1,950 in 1810 to 22,800 in 1825, and from 63,466 in 1835 to 78,533 in 1850. The number of admission tickets issued rose from less than 150 per annum in the period 1759–1810 to 3,000 in 1856, and it continued to rise thereafter by about 3,000 each year. By 1888 the number of printed books had grown to 1,500,000 – increasing at the rate of 26,000 volumes and 56,000 periodical parts per year. And in that year the number of readers' visits stood at more than 180,000. By 1889 the British Museum was issuing each year five times as many books as the Bibliothèque Nationale, to three times as many readers. Panizzi's dream had come true. Paris had been surpassed.

The library's phenomenal rate of growth was only made possible by a truly phenomenal building, the Round Reading Room. All through the 1840s there was talk of reconstruction. Congestion was acute. When the great Grenville Library arrived by bequest in 1847, its volumes had to be stacked on the floor of the manuscripts department. Books in the reserve stacks were crowded three deep on the shelves. The old reading rooms were crammed. Something had to be done. Schemes for expansion began to be prepared. And in April 1852, working late one evening in his office, Panizzi sketched out on a piece of scrap paper his vision of a circular library in the middle of the central quadrangle. The Round Reading Room was born.

But this was by no means the origin of the idea. Several precedents for a round or oval reading room already existed. There was, of course,

69 *(below)*. The Radcliffe Camera, Oxford (1737–49), James Gibbs

70 *(opposite left)*. Ground plan of the Imperial Library at St Petersburg (1795 onwards), Sotokoff and Rusco

71 *(opposite right)*. Ground plan of Duke Anton Ulrich's Library at Wolfenbüttel (1706–10), Hermann Korb

72 *(opposite below)*. George III's Library, Buckingham House (1766–8), Sir William Chambers

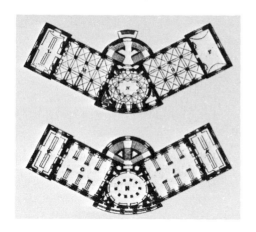

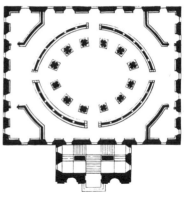

James Gibbs's circular Radcliffe Camera at Oxford (1737-49) [69]. Less obviously, there were also two Continental precedents: the oval central apartment of Sotokoff and Rusco's Imperial Library at St Petersburg (1795 onwards) [70]; and Duke Anton Ulrich's library at Wolfenbüttel (1706-10), designed by Hermann Korb as an oval set in a rectangle [71]. Moreover, George III's library had originally been housed in a domed, octagonal chamber [72] designed by Sir William Chambers in 1766-8 as an addition to old Buckingham House. Robert Adam's Register House, Edinburgh (1774-92), incorporated a circular library set in a quadrangular plan. So did visionary schemes by Boullée (1785), Durand (1802) and C. R. Cockerell, (Cambridge 1830). But all these were designed as classical, masonry structures. A much more significant precedent, in style, structure and plan, appeared in 1835.

In that year Benjamin Delessert, botanist, politician and bibliophile, published in Paris his *Mémoire sur la Bibliothèque Royale*. This attempted to apply Benthamite panopticon principles to the problems of the Royal Library, Paris. 'I propose', he wrote, 'to place the officers and readers in the centre of a vast rotunda, whence branch off eight principal galleries, the walls of which form diverging radii . . . and have book cases on both sides.' Delessert's circular library [73, 74], clothed in Italianate detailing was to have been constructed entirely of stone, marble, iron, pottery and zinc. It was to have been centrally heated, and lighted at clerestory level. It was designed to house 800,000 books, and was estimated at £330,000. Its layout differed in two important respects from the reading room which was eventually built in Bloomsbury. In the first place, readers were not distributed at radiating desks but, together with officers, were placed at the centre of the circle and were themselves surrounded by radiating bookshelves. In the second place, Delessert's circular structure was conceived in a spatial vacuum. As Count Leon de Laborde pointed out in *De L'Organisation des Bibliothèques dans Paris* (1845), it wasted the space in the four angles of any square within which it might be placed. He would himself have preferred to incorporate the

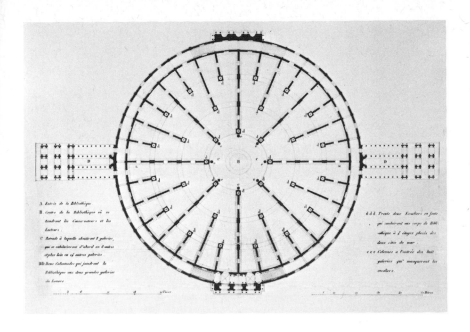

73, 74. Project for a Circular Royal Library, Paris (1835), Benjamin Delessert

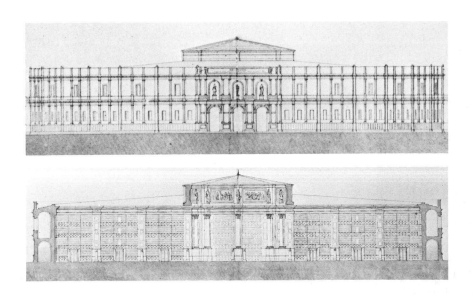

old buildings of the Mazarine Palace in an expanded cruciform layout: a cross set in a rectangle, rather on the lines of an earlier scheme by Visconti. At the British Museum de Laborde's objection was eventually answered by setting the round reading room within a rectangular bookstack. But as regards Delessert's scheme, there was initially no such problem: it was designed to occupy the Place du Carrousel, next to the Louvre and the Tuileries. When the Place Belle-Chasse was then put forward as a more suitable site, Delessert changed his approach and in 1838 produced his *Seconde Mémoire*, an ingenious adaptation of his first scheme, squeezing the panopticon plan into a rectangular space, and turning the circle into an oval [75]. In the end, neither of Delessert's projects was adopted. But such precedents can hardly have gone unnoticed on the other side of the channel.

For in the very year of Delessert's first *Mémoire* the British Museum entered one of its recurrent administrative and financial crises. A parliamentary committee was set up, and produced its report in 1836. The press was naturally filled with comments. And among these were two articles written by young Thomas Watts, Panizzi's future right-hand man. The first compared the British Museum library with the Royal Library at Paris, and concluded with the prophetic imperative: 'Paris must be surpassed!' The second suggested the installation of a reading room in the centre of Smirke's quadrangle.

This suggestion appeared, without a plan, in the *Mechanics' Magazine* for 11 March 1837, printed mysteriously over the initials P.P.C.R. Not until many years later was it revealed that these initials stood for 'Peerless Pool, City Road': the Watts family held shares in a swimming-bath. Watts curtly dismissed Smirke's empty quadrangle as 'a dead loss'. He put forward the idea of a central reading room bounded by bookstacks – cheaper than expanding along Montague Street, and less complicated than reviving Nash's dream of 1826 for redeveloping the area round St George's church. Now Watts did not specifically suggest a circular reading room. The room he had in mind might have been either round or

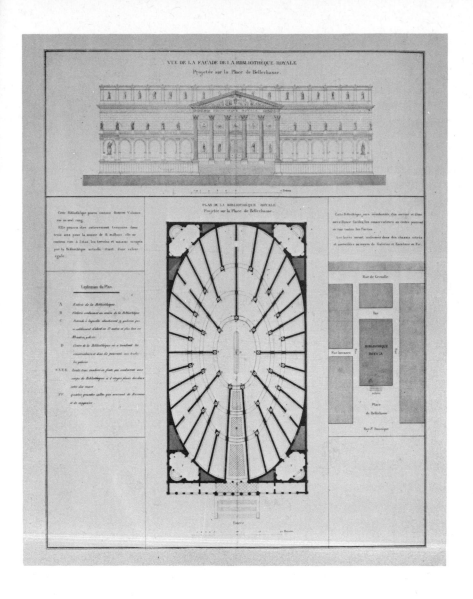

75. Revised Project for a Royal Library, Paris (1838), Benjamin Delessert

rectangular. The same held true for the next proposal, that of Edward Hawkins (1780-1867), Keeper of Antiquities, in 1842. He thought of filling the quadrangle with a central administrative building, linked by corridors to the four wings. And five years later, Edward Edwards trod much the same ground with a scheme included in his widely-read *Public Libraries in London and Paris* (1847). Apparently without knowledge of previous schemes, he suggested a new wing on the north side of the site, plus a rectangular linking wing across the centre of the quadrangle.

It was not until February 1848 that a specifically circular solution appeared. In that month William Hosking (1800-1861), Professor of Architecture at King's College London, prepared a scheme to present to the Parliamentary Commissioners then conducting one of their periodic inquiries into the museum's affairs. Thus began Hosking's private campaign to dwarf Sir Robert Smirke's quadrangle with his own design for a 'masonic Pantheon' or circular hall of antiquities [76A]. Submitted to the Trustees in November 1849, this circular central feature was to be bounded by an octagonal area for staircases and exhibition galleries. Hawkins seems to have supplied Hosking with a programme for rearranging books, manuscripts and sculptures. Hosking was himself better known as a railway engineer and an expert on building regulations. His most celebrated design was the West London Railway's three-decker road, rail and canal junction at Wormwood Scrubs, built by Cubitts at a cost of £7,680 (1838-9). As an architect, he favoured a rather austere, engineer's classicism. And his British Museum scheme, while admittedly impressive, must surely have seemed as grim as Brunel's project for the Great Exhibition, so happily defeated by Paxton. Hosking's scheme was not published till June 1850. Meanwhile, in 1849 James Fergusson had entered the lists with his swingeing *Observations on the British Museum, National Gallery and National Record Office*. Watts had suggested moving the antiquities to Trafalgar Square: 'the pictures have been removed, why should not the statues follow?' Fergusson now proposed not only the transfer of antiquities to the National Gallery, but

76. Three schemes for a new British Museum Reading Room:

(A) by William Hosking (1848–9);
(B) by Panizzi and Sydney Smirke (1852) and
(C) by Panizzi and Sydney Smirke (1854)

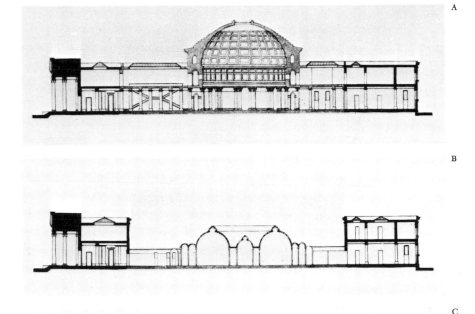

A

B

C

the removal of the natural history collections as well, and their replacement by the accumulated papers of the National Record Office. This was a new permutation. In 1832 Nash's schemes for the Trafalgar Square area had included a joint National Gallery and Record Office, on the site of Wilkins's future building. Fergusson's suggestion was rather more logical. By combining printed books and manuscripts on a grand scale, Bloomsbury would be transformed into 'the great repository of all the printed and written treasures of the nation'. And in Smirke's quadrangle could be placed a rectangular, glass-walled reading room for those consulting either books or manuscripts or both. It was a radical and exciting vision – too exciting and too radical to be considered seriously. Still more so, his long-term dream of reconstructing the whole museum as an expandable bookstack. The only precedent for such a basically utilitarian book-warehouse was the visionary project of the Florentine writer Leopoldo della Santa: *Della construzione e del regolamento di una universale biblioteca, con la pianta dimonstrativa* (Florence, 1816). This had been praised by Follini, Librarian of the Magliabecchiana, and by Molbech, Librarian of the Royal Library at Copenhagen. But it won little or no recognition in Britain. Fergusson's radical proposals were likewise airily discussed and then conveniently ignored.

In 1850 the *Civil Engineer and Architect's Journal* produced a much more conventional alternative, perhaps by W. H. Leeds (1786–1866): a scheme for a central hall of sculpture with an inner and outer rotunda modelled on the so-called Glyptotheca of Decimus Burton's Colosseum in Regent's Park. Such an idea was certainly less *outré* than Fergusson's. And at the end of nearly two decades of discussion, John and Wyatt Papworth accurately reflected a general aversion to extreme solutions by publishing in their influential *Museums, Libraries and Picture Galleries* (1853) a compromise, all-purpose public library programme prepared in 1852: a polygonal reading room, without radiating desks, surrounded by offices and expandable bookstacks. 'The polygonal form', they concluded, 'is not unsuitable.'

As for the use of cast iron, by the early 1850s precedents were legion. The structural use of the new material had been pioneered in eighteenth-century factories and bridges. Its decorative possibilities had been amply exploited during the Regency. In the early Victorian period cast iron emerged as one of the major determinants in the design of public buildings. The most striking precedents were the most recent. J. B. Bunning's domed Coal Exchange (1846-9) [77] had certainly shown London cast iron's decorative and structural potential. David Cousins's rectangular

77. The Coal Exchange, London (1846-9), J. B. Bunning

Corn Exchange (1847–9) performed a similar advertising function in Edinburgh. And Sir Joseph Paxton's Crystal Palace of 1851 had set all Europe talking: the logic of those soaring conservatories at Syon (Charles Fowler, 1827–30), at Chatsworth (Paxton and Burton, 1836–40) and at Kew Gardens (Burton and Turner, 1846–9) had been followed through to a glorious conclusion. Even before that great event, Fowler's Hungerford Market (1835) had already demonstrated the versatility of cast iron construction and prefabricated components. Even small commercial firms were making large-scale use of the new material: in 1843 David Mocatta designed a striking, iron-framed shop in Oxford Street. Abroad, Henri Labrouste's long reading room at the Bibliothèque Sainte Geneviève (designed 1839; built 1843–50) had combined a Neo-Renaissance exterior with iron-arched interior construction – a miniature Crystal Palace enclosed in stone [78]. T. N. Walker's new book-stack in the Library of Congress at Washington (1851–2) incorporated a fire-proof stone floor and massive use of iron shelving. But in exploiting cast iron

78. The reading room in the Bibliothèque Sainte Geneviève, Paris (designed 1839; built 1843–50), Henri Labrouste

it was of course the railway stations – English ones – which held the lead. Sir William Fairbairn's massive train shed at Liverpool Street Station was finished in 1850. In that year also work began on the construction of Paddington Station, a triple-arched masterpiece by a justly famous trio: an engineer, I. K. Brunel; an architect, Sir Matthew Digby Wyatt; and a decorator, Owen Jones. And as Paddington soared to completion in 1854, E. A. Cowper produced an even more astonishing, single-span structure at New Street Station, Birmingham. The 1850s were indeed an Age of Iron. And libraries seemed poised to repeat, in modified form, the triumphs of mid-Victorian engineering.

So there was no shortage of precedents when Panizzi got to work. As he admitted in 1859, 'schemes for covering over, or building in the quadrangle were numberless'. Several of them involved a circular apartment for antiquities or printed books, and nearly all implied the structural use of cast iron. Still, as Watts loyally pointed out, 'whoever may have suggested the proposition, it was only such a man as Mr Panizzi who would have got the project carried out'.

Panizzi's famous first sketch was drawn out rather more professionally by a draughtsman named Charles Cannon and laid before the Trustees in May 1852. The idea was then translated into architectural terms by Sydney Smirke, sanctioned by the Trustees, and presented to the Treasury in June. There it was initially rejected. And for some months the future of the Panizzi–Sydney Smirke project hung in the balance. Now this design did not yet incorporate the famous single dome. It consisted of several concentric galleries, supported on cast iron columns, covered with coved glazing and surrounded by a rectangular book-stack [76B]. Its merits were at best pedestrian. Hosking called it 'miserable as a scheme and miserable as a design'. But it would at least have been cheap: the estimate was £56,000. It was really no more than a development of the conservatory principle, bent into concentric formation. In conjunction with Thomas Prosser, Sydney Smirke's own father-in-law, John Dobson, had designed the great station at Newcastle, with its platform aisles curved in very similar fashion. The first Panizzi–Sydney Smirke scheme was opposed, therefore, not because of any structural novelty, but on grounds of long-term strategy.

In the first place, any use of the quadrangle was opposed by those who still clung to the hope of large-scale expansion towards Russell Square and Montague Street. This had been the course proposed in 1848 by Sydney Smirke and Panizzi themselves. In the second place, a rival scheme had been prepared by Sir Charles Barry (1795–1860), official architect of the Houses of Parliament. Sponsored by the Office of Works and by the editor of the *Quarterly Review*, John Wilson Croker, Barry's project combined the reconstruction of the north wing with 'preservation' of the quadrangle: the whole area was to have been glazed over in Crystal Palace fashion as a grandiose gallery of antiquities. 'We need not', Croker airily concluded, 'trouble ourselves with any details . . . the Crystal Palace has settled all such questions.'

Such an idea had already been put forward in the *Builder* in 1850, and it had certain obvious attractions. Panizzi and Sydney Smirke had themselves once toyed with a very similar scheme. But Barry's proposal also formed part of a much wider restructuring of London's cultural facilities: Prince Albert had already set in motion the redevelopment of South Kensington as a by-product of the Great Exhibition. Barry's scheme, presented to the Prince Consort in October 1853, was in fact a North London counter-project to the prospective concentration in the west. First, he repeated the suggestion that Natural History should be removed – this time to Kensington, to form part of a new Temple of Sciences or National Gallery of Science, in conjunction with the Jermyn Street Museum of Economic Geology. Then he suggested the removal to Bloomsbury of the treasures of the National Gallery and the Royal Society of Arts, to form a new British Museum of Art and Literature, leaving Wilkins's Trafalgar Square building as a new School of Design for Practical and Decorative Art. Needless to say, the scheme came to nothing. Albertopolis had already been launched, and the Victoria and

Albert Museum was not so easily strangled at birth. As Barry's son and biographer later remarked, the architect was in a way merely 'satisfying the imperious requirements of his architectural conscience'.

But Barry's scheme did hold out a last hope for Sir Robert Smirke's quadrangle: it might take on a new lease of life as a vast exhibition area. Croker – Smirke's old Tory supporter – leapt at the chance. With the *Quaterly Review* as a megaphone, he dismissed Panizzi's first 'panopticon reading room' as a 'monstrous scheme . . . four circles of gradually diminishing cupola-roofs, supported on iron pillars, and all . . . partaking of the arabesque character'. All in all it was 'a gigantic birdcage'. Barry's design, on the other hand, would preserve the grandeur of the quadrangle 'in its naked severity'. But there were undeniable constructional difficulties. Heat, light and fresh air would be formidably difficult to control. 'The more I consider it in detail', wrote Sydney Smirke, 'the more preposterous it seems.' When the controversy was limited to Bloomsbury, the whole dispute really revolved round the merits of keeping or abolishing a view of the quadrangle. To most critics that particular empty space was merely, in Grenville's words, 'the finest mason's yard in Europe'. To others it was still 'one of the grandest things in London'. In the end Treasury and Trustees bowed to the inevitable and recognized an eternal museological truth: museum buildings abhor a vacuum. The quadrangle had to be filled. Barry's scheme was rejected as gloomy, chilly and impractical, and in May 1854 work began at last on the new addition, now matured by Sydney Smirke and ready in its final form: a single-domed, circular reading room, set in an insulated rectangle and connected by corridors to the old north and south wings [76c].

And what did the aged Sir Robert Smirke have to say? No record survives of his reaction, far away among the gouty gentry of Bath. But he always had the greatest confidence in the work of his younger brother, 'little Sid'. And the fact that the new reading room made the plan of the British Museum more similar than ever to the Dublin Parliament House, may even have made the old man smile.

79. The Round Reading Room during construction (*c.* 1856).

The first brick was laid in September. Erection of the giant cast iron skeleton [79] began in the following January. All through 1855 and 1856 work continued at breakneck pace. In June 1855 the scaffolding was removed; in September the dome was covered with copper. Panizzi urged on the workmen with cries of 'zounds!' and 'Damn you, you shall not go till you haf finished.' By the spring of 1857 all was ready, and the bill totalled £150,000.

As the great dome soared upwards, the contest for its credit began. Delessert had died in 1847. Watts, Hawkins and Edwards remained loyal to Panizzi. And Fergusson stayed scornfully aloof. So there remained three chief contestants: Hosking, Panizzi and Sydney Smirke.

Hosking rushed into print first. He had never forgiven Sydney Smirke for inheriting Sir Robert Smirke's responsibility for the building of King's College – the very place where he himself held London's first chair of building science. Now he claimed that his scheme for the British Museum had been brazenly plagiarized – and plagiarized after it had been rejected. The *Building News* summed up the situation as follows:

failing the Royal Exchange, Mr Hosking's hopes were turned to the British Museum, when he found that the museum was getting very full, and that the authorities had just completed an area of an acre and three-quarters in the centre, which poor Sir Robert Smirke had intended for his own especial glorification, as an embodiment of the grand, chaste, simple and naked, but which Mr Hosking thought was meant for his dome.

Hosking saw the situation rather differently. 'Finding', he wrote, 'a barefaced plagiary established . . . I determined to ruffle, and, if I could, to pluck out the feathers which I believed to have been filched from me.' He dismissed the new reading room as 'a bad imitation' of his own scheme, 'as Guildhall Gog is to the Apollo Belvedere'. 'Nonsense!', noted Panizzi in the margin of Hosking's pamphlet; 'what a goose!'

Still, Panizzi cannot have been completely unaware of Hosking's scheme. Perhaps it would have been wiser if, like Sydney Smirke, he had candidly admitted seeing it. After all, Hosking's project was only one of several. And the reading room, as finally built, differed markedly – in proportion, structure and purpose – from Hosking's abortive design. But Panizzi's enthusiasm led him to claim far more than his fair share of responsibility. In this way he not only crossed swords with Hosking unnecessarily; he also impugned the reputation of the reading room's real architect, Sydney Smirke [80]. 'I have submitted a plan . . . to the Trustees', he told Lord Rutherford in May 1852, 'which has taken with

80. *Sydney Smirke*
(1798–1877),
Sculptor unknown.

them all amazingly . . . even the architect is pleased with it. He will have nothing on earth to do but carry into execution my ideas; he has not been able to suggest one single improvement.' When the room was opened most of the credit certainly went to Panizzi – as Hosking put it 'the gale [of approval] filled the pirate's sails'. And when Lord John Russell announced in the House of Commons that Panizzi was 'the first to suggest the erection of a building on so magnificent a scale', Hosking's fury knew no bounds. But the Professor blew his architectural trumpet in vain: all the credit for the reading room obstinately clung to its librarian.

Hosking died in 1861, but the controversy was by no means finished. And when in 1866, in the House of Commons, Robert Lowe referred to

Panizzi as 'the architect', Sydney Smirke thought it was time to set the record straight. 'Briefly', he wrote to *The Times*,

the facts are these: some years ago the late Professor of Architecture at King's College suggested building a circular, domed hall for sculpture in the quadrangle. Some years afterwards Mr Panizzi suggested building a flat, low circular reading room in the same place. The Trustees did me the honour to consult me, and I quite approved of Mr Panizzi's suggestion, but proposed a dome and glazed vaulting, to give more air to the readers and a more architectural treatment to the interior. This grew, on maturer consideration, into the much larger dome as erected . . . For the arrangement and form of a great number of interior details I had the invaluable advantage of the direct instructions of the Principal Librarian . . . Every aesthetic merit, however, that the reading room may possess I claim as literally and exclusively my own.

On another occasion Sydney Smirke had to remind Panizzi that 'the architectural features [windows, rib-vaulting, gliding etc.] of the present dome I am answerable for, not you. . . . It was Michael Angelo's cupola of St Peter's which suggested the present lines' – so different both to Panizzi's low-scaled domical structure and to Hosking's reproduction of the Pantheon. Years later, in Panizzi's obituary, *The Times* made amends by describing him, very properly, as the 'originator' of the Round Reading Room. So justice was done in the end – except for the neglect of one man's memory, a Frenchman named Benjamin Delessert.

The new reading room was opened in May 1857 with a formal breakfast ceremonially eaten off the catalogue desks. The dome instantly became one of the sights of London. First of all, its sheer size was impressive: it contained some $1\frac{1}{4}$ million cubic feet of space. Its diameter was 140 feet, as against only 120 feet in Hosking's scheme and 75 feet in that of Leeds. And the newspapers recorded with relish the smaller dimensions of its rivals: St Peter's, Rome and S. Maria Novella, Florence, 139 feet; the tomb of Mahomet at Bejapore, 135 feet; St Paul's London, 112 feet; S. Sophia, Constantinople, 107 feet; Möller's church at Darm-

81. Comparative cross sections
on the Pantheon, Rome *(left)* and the Round Reading Room *(right)*

stadt, 105 feet. Only the Pantheon remained unequalled, with a diameter
of 143 feet [81] – and the critics hastened to add that whereas the masonry
piers supporting the Pantheon occupied some 7,477 square feet of space,
those of the Round Reading Room occupied only 200 square feet. Then
there was the ingenuity of its construction – directed by Sydney Smirke,
watched over by Panizzi, guarded by Dennison the Clerk of Works, and
executed by the contractors Baker and Fielder, the heating engineers
Heydon of Trowbridge, and Pontifex the suppliers of metal work. The
great dome was entirely carried on cast iron ribs. The main member of
each girder was of I-section with its web radial to the dome. Two smaller
I-sections, with their webs at right angles to that of the main member,

82. Tables and chairs in the Round Reading Room

were bolted together through holes in the main web. No attempt was made to fit the three members together. Instead, gaps were deliberately left between the castings. And these were filled not with lead but with 'rust cement', a paste invented by William Murdoch (1754–1839), consisting of iron filings, sal-ammoniac and water. This swelled as it set and, with the bolts, bound the three uprights into a single girder of cruciform section. In all, the construction of reading room and bookstacks involved 2,000 tons of iron and provided 25 miles of shelving for 1,300,000 books. Sydney Smirke designed the leather and mahogany chairs [82], Panizzi the galvanized iron bookshelves and padded reading desks. The floor was raised on brick arches filled out with Portland cement, smoothed over with Bellman's Parian cement and then covered with kamptulicon, a sound-absorbing material composed of cork and india-rubber. The mouldings of the dome were worked in 'patent wood or fibrous slab'. The clerestory windows and central 'hypaethric light' were filled with 60,000 square feet of double glazing.

But it was the complicated system of heating and ventilation which aroused most admiration. Each reader was supplied with warming pipes for his feet and air vents in each table. *The Times* carried a detailed description of the process:

the air chamber below [floor level] . . . is six feet high and occupies the whole area of the reading room. It is fitted with hot water pipes arranged in radiating lines. The supply of fresh air is obtained from a shaft 60 ft. high, built on the North side of the North wing about 300 ft. distant, communicating with a tunnel or subway, which has branches or 'loop-lines' fitted with valves for diverting the current, either wholly through the heating apparatus, or through the cold-air flues, or partly through either . . . The air chambers are of sufficient capacity to admit a supply of fresh air for 500 persons at the rate of 10 cubic feet per minute, and at a velocity not exceeding one foot per second. For summer ventilation steam pipes, placed at the summit of the roof and dome, will be heated, and extract the foul air . . . The roof is formed into two separate spherical and concentric air chambers extending over the whole surface – one between the external covering and brick vaulting, the object of which is the equalisation of temperature during extremes of heat and cold out of doors; the other between the brick vaulting and the internal visible surface, and which is intended to carry off the vitiated air from the reading room. This ventilation is partly affected through apertures in the soffits of the windows, and partly through others at the top of the dome, the bad air passing through outlets provided around the lantern. The effects of condensation are obviated by making all the skylights, lanterns and windows throughout the building double . . .

In 1851 the *Athenaeum* had protested against such a monstrous room: 'No man can *write* well at the Museum, and not one in ten can *read* to any good purpose. What would it be if there were 500 persons coughing, scribbling, rocking, stamping, walking, talking, laughing, sneezing,

83. A fish-eye view of the Round Reading Room

snoring, fumbling, grumbling, mumbling – all in one miscellaneous chorus?' But by 1857 even such a cacophony as this would have been drowned by the chorus of approval in the press.

With the opening of the Round Reading Room [83], Sydney Smirke's reputation was made. He was already well known as a competent Gothicist, the man who restored the nave of York Minster (1840–44) and reconstructed the Temple Church in London (1840–43). He was already acknowledged as a master of Italianate classicism, second only to Sir Charles Barry – after all he had designed the new Carlton Club in Pall Mall (1847–56), as well as that 'King of Clubs', the Conservative Club in St James's (1843–5). Now he had also proved his mastery of large-scale cast iron construction. The award of the R.I.B.A. Gold Medal followed inevitably in 1860. As an exercise in the architectural use of cast iron the Round Reading Room seemed a massive prophecy of still greater things to come. 'Cast iron', the architect remarked, 'perfectly satisfies me of its excellence as a building material.' And it has satisfied posterity too. Except in 1907, when the collapse of the barrel roof at Charing Cross station produced a wave of panic among surveyors, there has never been any serious doubt as to the reading room's structural soundness. In a sense, the Round Reading Room has always been Bloomsbury's answer to Paddington station: a mighty vote of confidence in Victorian technology.

And yet, Sydney Smirke's whole conception on this occasion was based on an aesthetic compromise: the absorption of new materials and new structural techniques into an inherited stylistic framework. Style, he openly admitted, had become merely a regularized system of expressive ornament. The structural premises of both the Gothic and Classic traditions had become outdated; their purpose had become primarily evocative and disciplinary. Circumstances had changed and yet no new style had emerged. 'Architecture', he used to tell his Royal Academy pupils, 'has not kept pace with time.' And the only future he held out to his professional juniors was 'a long purgatorial period of folly and excess', an 'eclectic or latitudinarian' interlude, leading – with luck – to 'a sound, consistent and original style, worthy of the genius and civilization of the nineteenth century'. Such indecision, such confused optimism, is clearly visible in the stylistic vocabulary of his Round Reading Room. The giant iron ribs of the dome dictate their own symmetry. The formalized pattern of the galleries – happily echoing the chequering of the great oculus – has the right metallic formation. The only weaknesses of the whole design lie at the points where it compromises the logic of its construction: the Lombardic fenestration of the clerestory; the interpenetration of drum and dome; the false bookcases masking each rib at lower level. Such compromises can occasionally be carried off with panache. After all, even the peaks of High Victorian achievement were sometimes shot through with compromise. But in the hands of lesser architects compromise hovers on the brink of platitude. And, sitting in the Round Reading Room of the British Museum, it is hard to resist the conclusion that Professor Sydney Smirke, R.A., was a first-rate constructor but no more than a first-class, second-rate architect.

Perhaps this impression is at least partly due to the reading room's incomplete decoration. The present decorative scheme represents only part of Sydney Smirke's intention. Despite Panizzi's opposition, he insisted on divided windows rather than plain rectangular openings; a visible ribbing rather than concealed supports; and a generous gilding to 'illuminate, as it were, the whole building'. But his dream of completing the decorative programme with painting and statuary remained unfulfilled. The Round Reading Room was to have continued an ancient tradition of inspirational decoration in library design. Allegorical paintings and portrait sculptures were to have reminded readers of the triumphs of past literature. Each massy console at cornice level was to have carried a marble statue. Each of the dome's twenty panels was to have framed a pictorial symbol. And the artist chosen was worthy of the commission: Alfred Stevens – in Christopher Hussey's words, 'the last of the great humanist artists'.

84. Design for the decoration of the Round Reading Room, Alfred Stevens

The year of the Round Reading Room's opening was also competition
year for the Wellington memorial in St Paul's Cathedral. That famous
monument – by which Stevens will always be remembered – was never
finished, though the artist laboured at it for nearly twenty years. By comparison his scheme for the reading room was scarcely even begun. It
progressed no further than the construction of a model showing the
distribution of decorative paintings across the dome: one branch of
man's creative achievement – Painting, Poetry, Chemistry, Physics,
Jurisprudence, Theology, Mathematics etc. – in each of the twenty bays
[84]. In the horizontal arrangement of portraits and *putti*, subtly counter-
acting the verticality of the ribbing, there are faint but recognizable
echoes of the Sistine Chapel. But, as so often in Stevens's career, his
boldly Michaelangelesque designs remained . . . designs. Both Treasury

85. Design for the decoration of the Round Reading Room, Sigismund Goetze

and Trustees seemed reluctant to sanction further spending – though an engineer named Volprignano did produce a system of scaffolding in 1864, designed to allow the work to be completed without disturbing readers. And even had the money been forthcoming, the artist himself would almost certainly have killed the project by procrastination. Stevens suffered acutely from an obsessional and perfectionist temperament. He dressed like a priest and lived like a hermit. He kept peacocks in his study and a tiny pet dog in his breast pocket. 'To the grief of his admirers' – so runs *The Times*'s obituary – 'he was most impracticable. He was never satisfied with his work, he would destroy model after model and sketch after sketch while he was eating only a crust of bread. Indeed, unless the work was dragged from him, he would never have finished it or given it up . . . He . . . left neither wife, nor children, nor riches, but the name of one of the greatest decorative artists, insanely devoted to his art.' And the empty dome of the reading room must surely rank as one of the greatest of Stevens's lost opportunities.

The very emptiness of Bloomsbury's vast dome remained a standing provocation to decorative artists. But after Stevens's death only one painter came near to abolishing its vacuity, Sigismund Goetze (1866–1939). Besides being a fashionable portrait, landscape and historical painter, Goetze was himself something of a Maecenas. In fact he is better remembered today as a patron than as an artist. But his work in one public building – on the great staircase of the Foreign Office in Whitehall – is still very much in the public eye. At the Royal Academy banquet of 1912 the Archbishop of Canterbury had criticized the 'drab, uninspiring surroundings of our officials'. Goetze replied by decorating Gilbert Scott's Italianate building free of charge, with frescoes symbolic of the origin, development and expansion of the British Empire. But his similar offer to decorate the reading room was politely declined. Goetze was a strong admirer of Alfred Stevens, and his allegorical schemes [85] for Sydney Smirke's dome clearly owe something to his predecessor's designs. But whereas Stevens emphasized the diameter of the room, Goetze emphasized its height.

Either way, the reading room's decoration remained a dream. The dome's vast proportions remained unexploited. Instead four neutral schemes – gilded features against pastel shades of cream, white and blue – have followed each other, each more simple than the last, in 1856, 1907, 1952 and 1963–4. Only the redecoration of 1907 by Waring and Gillow, made any attempt at novelty. In that year, under Sir John Burnet's direction, the names of nineteen British writers were painted on the panels above the cornice – a meagre apology for Stevens's absent statues. For almost half a century, growing gradually more faded until they were eventually obliterated, these ghosts of the great looked down upon their literary descendants like the spectres in Geoffrey Crayon's dream. The choice of names evoked some controversy at the time and is perhaps worth recording: Chaucer, Caxton, Tindale, Spenser, Shakespeare, Bacon, Milton, Locke, Addison, Swift, Pope, Gibbon, Wordsworth, Scott, Byron, Carlyle, Macaulay, Tennyson and Browning.

The prestige of the Round Reading Room influenced library planning all over the world. Only a few examples need mentioning. The circular reading rooms of the Library of Congress (finished 1897) [86], the Prus-

86. The circular reading room in the Library of Congress, Washington, D.C.

sian State Library (finished 1914); and the State Library at Stockholm – all these trace their ancestry to Bloomsbury. So do the round room at London's Public Record Office (designed by Sir James Pennethorne, 1851-66), the circular Picton Reading Room in Liverpool (1875-9, by Cornelius Sherlock), Manchester Central Library (1930-34, by E. Vincent Harris), and the circular Brotherton Library at Leeds University (Lan-

87. Salle de Travail, Bibliothèque Nationale (1862-8), Henri Labrouste

chester, Lucas and Lodge, 1936). But from Panizzi's point of view, perhaps the most flattering instance of imitation occurred in Paris. In 1854
Henri Labrouste succeeded Visconti as government architect, and began
the reconstruction of the future Bibliothèque Nationale. Besides adapt-
ing the older buildings, the Hôtel de Tuboeuf and the Galerie Mazarine,
he installed a fine new library at the junction of the Rue des Petits Champs
and the Rue de Richelieu, with an entrance on to the Place Louvois. It
boasted two major features: the metal stacked *magasin*, and the Salle de
Travail, opened 1868 [87]. Both contained echoes of Bloomsbury. The
magasin reproduced the principles of the Iron Library. The Salle de
Travail, although oblong, was very much a librarian's vote of confidence
in cast iron, and it did have an apsidal recess at one end. And, just to
complete the picture, the Bibliothèque Nationale opened a new periodi-

cals room in 1936 – the Salle Ovale. Many reading rooms in many countries must be haunted by Panizzi's ghost.

The Round Reading Room has received many tributes, but none more eloquent than Thackeray's. In a *Roundabout Paper*, 'Nil nisi bonum', he wrote in 1862:

I have seen all sorts of domes of Peters and Pauls, Sophia, Pantheon – what not? – and have been struck by none of them as much as by that catholic dome in Bloomsbury, under which our million volumes are housed. What peace, what love, what truth, what beauty, what happiness for all, what generous kindness for you and me are here spread out! It seems to me one cannot sit down in that place without a heart full of grateful reverence. I own to have said my grace at the table, and to have thanked Heaven for this my English birthright, freely to partake of these beautiful books, and speak the truth I find there.

Even if the rest of the museum succumbs to the virus of admission charges, the British Museum library must surely always remain free.

6: Crisis

'The Government . . . has put Bloomsbury
. . . in the gallery of non-stop planning follies'
(*The Times*, 27 October 1967)

Between the 1860s and the 1960s, the British Museum existed in a state of almost continuous crisis. Short of space and starved of funds, its building programme was at best spasmodic. And each new spasm has seemed more convulsive than the last. Architecturally, the Round Reading Room was the antithesis of Sir Robert Smirke's original scheme. But its installation followed logically from the principle of the museum's foundation. It was an expedient adopted to perpetuate the eighteenth-century dream of a multi-purpose treasure house. In fact almost the whole of the museum's architectural history has consisted of repeated attempts to maintain this comprehensive principle against the disintegrative forces of specialization. Hence the atmosphere of crisis which has haunted several generations of Trustees.

This prolonged crisis has been both financial and physical. Internationally speaking, the purchasing power of the British Museum reached its peak in the 1870s. Since then there has been a steady decline. For example, Panizzi's annual grant of £10,000 for purchases by the Department of Printed Books was cut in 1897 to £6,600, and remained at this level – despite inflation until 1928-30. In 1949-53 the Standing Commission on Museums and Galleries reported that the situation had become 'profoundly disquieting'. The annual Treasury grant for the whole museum has therefore been progressively raised. Even so, the museum's relative purchasing power has deteriorated still further. Its current total grant of £3,398,000 per annum, including £632,000 for purchases by all departments, places it well below a number of Continental and transatlantic museums. In short, a new economic situation has called into question two of the basic principles of the museum's foundation: free admission and perpetual expansion.

During the last century or so, with resources which – proportionately, at least – diminish with each succeeding year, the British Museum has had to struggle hard to keep afloat. In the first place the number of visitors has grown alarmingly. On Monday, 2 January 1843, the *Athenaeum* noted approvingly that in one day 'no less than 30,000 persons visited this National Establishment! The conduct of all was orderly, and there was not one single instance of drunkenness or indecorum.' In 1851, the year of the Great Exhibition, Bloomsbury attracted more than 1,000,000 visitors – more than the entire residential population of central London. That, of course, was exceptional. But even in normal years the flood continued to increase. By the end of the 1960s, the annual number of visitors had risen to nearly 2,000,000.

So popularity was one problem. Another was the sheer quantity of exhibits. And this raised a fundamental issue of principle. As late as 1835 H. S. Peacock, a surgeon with a taste for polemics, was still singing the praises of the unitary approach:

Man by nature is disposed to imitation . . . thereby displaying a creative power, which renders him a faint and feeble emblem of the Great Cause of all existence. This propensity he may exercise on the sublimest [level], by forming an assemblage of the most striking objects of nature and of art; thus representing in a museum the glories of the terrestial sphere, . . . a microcosm, or world in miniature. Such a Museum would constitute a noble Temple of Science . . . an honourable monument of national intelligence. . . . A national museum . . . should . . . be . . . a repository for all the available productions of nature and art. . . . According to this plan the National Gallery of Pictures would be included, and not constitute a separate institution. Antiquities should not constitute a separate section. . . . The whole should bespeak a *Lucidus ordo*, by which separate parts of the collection explain each other . . . commencing with the simplest productions of nature, and concluding with the library of books, the most perfect productions of man. . . . Thus a mineral may be considered an organised element; a vegetable a vitalised mineral; and an animal an animated vegetable . . . [Thus] the main object of classification . . . [is to] typify . . . nature, enlarging our conceptions of the universe . . . and shewing how [all] creation is single, connected and influenced by one law.

As an argument, it is logical enough. But its architectural implications are, quite literally, fantastic. Peacock absolves himself from such mundane considerations, and merely concludes: 'an appropriate building is also essential.'

As the Victorian years rolled on the pace of accumulation grew faster. And it was a cumulative process consciously fostered by the sponsoring of research at home and excavation abroad. By the 1860s the situation was once more acute. Layard's Assyrian discoveries, Fellowes's Lycian marbles, Rawlinson's Assyrian sculptures, Newton's discoveries in Asia Minor – Britain's museum waxed fat in prestige and congestion. As Edward Edwards boasted proudly in 1870: 'its contents . . . have come from the four quarters of the globe. . . . It brings together the plants of Australia; the minerals of Peru; the shells of the far Pacific; the manuscripts . . . painfully compiled or transcribed by twenty generations of labourers in every corner of Europe, as well as in the monasteries of Africa and of the Eastern Desert; and the sculptures and the printed books of every civilised country in the world.' 'We live in the era of *Omnium Gatherum*', wrote Robert Kerr in 1864; 'all the world's a museum, and men and women are its students.'

But in Bloomsbury the microcosm had become a mirage. Quite simply, there was not enough space. By 1875, according to the *Building News*, the museum had degenerated into 'a gigantic warehouse of unpacked goods', with specimens huddled together in the basement and sculptures crowded ignominiously inside penthouses in the colonnade. 'As the collection was made upon no principle,' it concluded, 'so its depository was constructed upon no plan.' But the *Building News* rather missed the point. The British Museum had both a principle and a plan. Unfortunately its plan was less elastic than its principle.

Here indeed was the nub of the problem. *The Times* summed it up nicely in 1852: 'The original conception of the British Museum, as it sprung from the mind of the Trustees a quarter of a century since, was a vast imperishable quadrangle in the most severely classic style, to serve as a monumental treasury of books, marbles and all sorts of curiosities. The building was to last as long as the Pyramids . . . being more fitted for preserving than for showing its contents.' By the end of its first century the scope of Britain's museum had not changed, but its scale had expanded enormously. Many must have sympathized with James Fergusson when he roundly condemned Smirke's portico as a museological straitjacket, an incubus preventing further expansion: thirsting for knowledge, he complained, 'we are chained, Tantalus-like, to the pillars of our Museum'.

Scarcely had the Round Reading Room been completed, when the problem of expanding accommodation for other departments was again raised. As before in 1848, so again in 1857, Sydney Smirke suggested building around the periphery of his brother's quadrangle. 'Feeling very averse to the idea of dismembering the Museum, and believing that, so far from its having become an overgrown establishment, it is by no means yet commensurate with the greatness of the country', he also suggested another alternative: adding a third storey on top of the original building. Neither proposal was implemented. In the end, an even more drastic solution was adopted – decentralization. The natural history collections were moved elsewhere.

But first came one last attempt to maximize gallery space on the existing site. Two small spaces still remained unused: the area to the north of the Nereid Room; and the Director's back garden. On these two sites were built the Mausoleum Room and the White Wing (1880–84). Both these additions were made possible by a belated bequest of

£65,411 from the estate of William White (d. 1823). The architect responsible was not a member of the Smirke family, but Sir John Taylor (1833–1912), Surveyor of Royal Palaces and Public Buildings in the Office of Works from 1866 to 1898. Taylor was a civil servant's architect, competent, prolific, dependable, and by no means squeamish about style. In his official capacity he designed or completed a remarkable assortment of metropolitan buildings: the War Office, Whitehall (Renaissance, 1898 and 1907); additions to Marlborough House (Wrenaissance, 1886); Bow Street Police Station (Palladian, 1899); the Chancery Lane front of the Public Record Office (Gothic, 1892–6); the Patent Office extension (Jacobethan, 1891–1902); the main staircase and central rooms at the National Gallery (mixed classic, 1884–7); and the Bankruptcy Courts in Carey Street (Italianate, 1890–92); as well as Bloomsbury's Mausoleum Room and White Wing, in chastest Greek Revival.

The creation of a separate Natural History Museum was a painfully slow process. Briefly, the story runs as follows. In 1856 the Zoological Society made over to the British Museum the contents of its own museum in Regent's Park. This made the problem of accomodating the natural history sections even more acute. Hence Sydney Smirke's suggestions in the following year. As early as 1853, however, the idea of a transfer to South Kensington had been aired for the first time. Inquiries as to a suitable site were set on foot in 1859. The scheme was sanctioned by the Trustees in 1860, but was then rejected by the House of Commons on grounds of expense. Thus the chance of using at least part of that sombre Romanesque fun palace, the 1862 Exhibition Building, was thrown away. However in 1863 part of the site occupied by the Exhibition was acquired – some twelve acres in all – and the machinery of architectural competition was set in motion. During 1862 specimen plans had been prepared by H. A. Hunt of the Office of Works, in conjunction with Professor Richard Owen, later first Superintendent of the Natural History Museum. These plans formed the basis of all subsequent designs. The competition judges were Lord Elcho, Sir William Tite, Sir James

Pennethorne and David Roberts, R.A. They unanimously awarded first prize to Captain Francis Fowke (1823–65) of the Royal Engineers, architect and engineer to the Science and Art Department, and the man responsible for a good deal of South Kensington's transformation into 'Albertopolis'.

However, Fowke's arrangements did not please the Trustees; and while he was inserting amendments he died, in September 1865. Early in 1866 Alfred Waterhouse was invited to execute Fowke's plan. He considered the offer for a while, and then declined. So, after some months of manoeuvring, Waterhouse was eventually commissioned, in February 1868, to produce his own design. In 1871 his plans were formally approved by the Trustees. And building finally began in 1873. But the new galleries were not finished until 1880. Only in 1886 was the new Natural History Section of the British Museum at last fully opened to the public – nearly thirty years after the division of the collections had first been mooted. The move to Kensington had cost more than £400,000.

As regards architectural style, the contrast between the parent museum and its offspring could hardly have been more dramatic. Smirke and Waterhouse were poles apart. The chastity of Bloomsbury was forgotten. Kensington's temple of science was to be Romanesque-Gothic. The brutal confidence of the style may surprise us now, but in the 1860s and 1870s such a choice was by no means unexpected. The classical temple – palazzo format dominated museum design in this country at the beginning of the nineteenth century and at its end. But in the middle, in the High Victorian period, the influence of Ruskin and the prestige of the natural sciences combined to break up the classical mystique. Ruskinian Gothic, with its wealth of naturalistic carving, its profusion of plants and animals carved in stone or cast in metal, seemed almost to embody the triumph of Darwinian principles.

This change of direction in museum design, from classic to Gothic, first occurred at Oxford. Begun in 1855, to designs by Benjamin Woodward, the Oxford Museum [88] was the first major museum in this coun-

88. The Oxford Museum (begun 1855), Sir T. Dean and B. Woodward

89. Natural History Museum, South Kensington, Sir Alfred Waterhouse

try to abandon classical conventions. Initially at any rate, it also represented a victory for the principles of John Ruskin, the theories of his *Seven Lamps of Architecture* and the precedents of his *Stones of Venice*. In its multitude of details the Oxford Museum pursues a major theme in Victorian museology: symbolism. The building was designed to contain a museum of science and lecture rooms, laboratories and libraries as well. The structure itself sought to reflect the scientific purposes it was built to serve: each column inside is hewn from an important British stone; each carving represents a different plant, flower or fruit, all arranged in natural sequence, and labelled. Hence the stylistic breakthrough. Classical culture cried out for a formal classical design. But a natural history museum lent itself admirably to the structural variety and decorative symbolism of Gothic. The only Gothic museum contemporary with Woodward's design is G. E. Street's Adderley Park Library and Museum in Birmingham. But Gilbert Scott soon followed with the Fitzroy Museum and Library at Lewes (1862), and the Albert Institute, Dundee (1867-73). Derby acquired a Gothic museum in 1879 and Manchester in 1888. And Venetian Gothic reappeared in Hayward's Royal Albert Memorial Museum, Gallery and Library in Exeter (1865-9); and in Ponton and Foster's City Museum, Bristol (1872). Another provincial example is F. R. Kempson's museum, art gallery and public library at Hereford (1872-5). But for the Victorian Gothic museum on the grand scale we must look to the metropolis.

During the century since their design, the Natural History galleries in Kensington [89, 90] have seemingly defied serious architectural criticism. At the time, their aggressive style was taken for granted. Then came the reaction: Augustus Hare called the building 'a huge pile of mongrel Lombardic architecture, an embodiment of portentous ugliness'. Later on, critics took refuge in parody, and flippantly agreed among themselves that Waterhouse could turn the strongest stomachs. Now at last the time seems ripe to revaluate his achievement. First of all, let Mr Waterhouse speak for himself:

The New Natural History Museum will, from its position, always be more or less identified with the International Exhibition of 1862, which occupied the whole of the site between the Horticultural Gardens and Cromwell Road. . . . In designing the present building, Captain Fowke's original idea of employing terra-cotta was always kept in view, though the blocks were reduced in size, so as to obviate, as far as possible, the objection to the employment of this material, arising from its liability to twist in burning. For this and other reasons the architect abandoned the idea of a Renaissance building, and fell back on the earlier Romanesque style which prevailed largely in Lombardy and the Rhineland from the tenth to the end of the twelfth century. . . . On looking at the exterior of the building, one of the first points which strikes the spectator is that the site is lower than the street. This arises from the fact that the whole surface of the ground between the three roads was excavated for the Exhibition building of 1862, and it was not thought desirable, for economical considerations, to refill the space. The building is set back 100 feet from the Cromwell Road, and is approached by two inclined planes, curved on plan and supported by arches, forming carriage-ways. Between the two are broad flights of Cragleith stone steps, for the use of those approaching the building on foot. The extreme length of the front is 675 feet, and the height of the towers . . . which in the first instance it was decided to omit . . . is 192 feet. The return fronts, east and west, beyond the end pavilions, have not yet been erected. [And] in judging the appearance of the exterior of the building, it must never be forgotten that these fronts are required to complete the design, as the externally unsightly brick galleries which run back from the main front, and are now conspicuous when the Museum is seen from either west or east, are intended to be concealed by them.

On entering the main portal, the visitor has before him the great central apartment of the Museum (170 feet long, by 97 feet wide, and 72 feet high), which it is intended to use an an Index or Typical Museum. The double arch in the immediate foreground which spans the nave (57 feet wide), carries the staircase from the second floor. Opposite the spectator, at the end of the hall, is the first flight of the staircase, 20 feet wide, which rises from the ground to the first floor. The galleries over the side recesses form the connection between the two staircases, and are also intended for exhibition space, as are also the floor of the main hall and the side recesses under the galleries. The arches under the side lights of the main staircase at the end of the hall lead into another large apartment, cruciform on

90. Main entrance of the Natural History Museum

plan, intended for the exhibition of specimens of British Natural History, with an extreme length of 97 by 77 feet measured into the arms of the cross.

Branching out of the Central Hall, near its southern extremity, are two long galleries, each 278 feet 6 in. long by 50 feet wide. These galleries are repeated on the first floor, and in a modified form on the second floor. They are divided into bays by coupled piers arranged in two rows down the length of the galleries, and planned in such a manner as to allow of upright cases being placed back to back between the piers and the outer walls, so as to get the best possible light upon the objects displayed in the cases with the least amount of reflection from the glass, and leaving the central space free as a passage. Owing to the nature of the specimens exhibited in one or two of these galleries requiring for their exhibition rather table-cases than wall-cases, advantage has only been taken to a limited extent of this disposition of the plan. These terra-cotta piers, however, are constructively necessary, not only to conceal the iron supports for the floor above, but to prevent these supports being affected in case of fire. Behind these galleries on the ground floor are a series of toplighted galleries, devoted on the east side to Geology and Palaeontology, and on the west to Zoology.

The towers on the north of the building have each a central smoke-shaft from the heating apparatus, the boilers of which are placed in the basement, immediately between the towers, while the space surrounding the smoke-shafts is used for drawing off the vitiated air from the various galleries contiguous thereto. The front galleries are ventilated into the front towers, which form the crowning feature of the main front. These towers also contain, above the second floor, various rooms for the work of the different heads of departments, and on the topmost storey large cisterns for the purpose of always having at hand a considerable storage of water in case of fire. On the western side of the building, where it is intended that the Zoological collection shall be placed, the ornamentation of the terra-cotta (which will be found very varied both within and without the building) has been based exclusively on living organisms. On the east side, where Geology and Palaeontology finds a home, the terra-cotta ornamentation has been derived from extinct specimens.

The Museum is the largest, if not, indeed, the only modern building in which terra-cotta has been extensively used for external facades and interior wall-surfaces, including all the varied decoration which this involves.

There it is, Waterhouse's credo, in prose as unemotive as his building is histrionic: functional planning; a technologist's pride in the capacity of his materials; the confidence of a born eclectic in the virtues of historicism; and a faith in the value of symbolic ornament only possible in the age of Ruskin. The terra-cotta animals – modelled by Du Jardin and supplied by Gibbs and Canning of Tamworth – even included, at Professor Huxley's suggestion, a statue of Adam on the apex of the central gable. This represented 'Man: the greatest beast of all'. But in the long catalogue of Waterhouse designs, the Natural History Museum cannot rank among his very best. In many of his works – preeminently at Manchester Town Hall (1868–77) – he held three trump cards: masterly planning, variegated silhouette and decorative fluency. At Kensington however, his planning was no more than adequate, his silhouette monotonous and his decorative detail repetitious. Only the sheer drama of its central hall raises the Natural History Museum to the highest level.

The galleries in South Kensington soon stretched to nearly four acres of exhibition space – apart from the laboratories, workshops, libraries and studies attached to their five departments: Zoology, Entomology, Palaeontology, Mineralogy and Botany. Here, perhaps more clearly than anywhere else in the British Museum, the three main purposes of any great museum could be seen in simultaneous operation: conservation, research and education. It was the second Superintendent and first Director, Sir William Flower (1831–99), who was chiefly responsible for initiating this museological breakthrough. It was he who established the separation of exhibition and study collections; the creation of an explanatory 'Index Museum' in the main hall; the introduction of instructional labels and graphic commentaries; and the fabrication of the earliest dioramas or environmental tableaux – setting animals in their natural habitat rather than 'skating on sycamore tables'. In all these ways, by the end of the nineteenth century, Kensington was teaching Bloomsbury a lesson. Soon there were 400,000 visitors a year. In 1896 the Natural History Museum was for the first time opened on a Sunday – in the same year as the British Museum proper. And during the twentieth century the Natural History Museum has steadily increased in reputation and popularity – culminating in the announcement in 1970 of a new £1,350,000 wing, designed by Mr J. A. H. Pearce of the Ministry of Public Buildings and Works.

The foundation of the Natural History Museum was the second major break in the Bloomsbury microcosm – the creation of the National Gallery [37] was the first. As early as 1824 Sir Robert Peel admitted to Sir Humphry Davy 'that, what with marbles, butterflies, statues, manuscripts, books and pictures, I think the museum is a farrago that distracts attention'. By 1845 Count Leon de Laborde, in *De l'Organisation des Bibliothèques dans Paris*, could dismiss the British Museum's unitary dream as 'a childish hope'. Imagine, he wrote, the folly of trying to combine the Louvre with the Jardin des Plantes, the École des Arts et Métiers, the École de l'Artillerie, the Hôtel de Cluny, and the Bibliothèque Royale. The result would be an administrative nightmare. As it was, Bloomsbury had merely become 'un pêle-mêle inextricable, une confusion fâcheuse'. By the later nineteenth century decentralization seemed the only answer.

And so, slowly but surely, the centrifugal pressure of specialization eroded the comprehensive principle. Paintings received their separate depository in 1825, natural history specimens in 1883, newspapers in 1905. Ethnography has teetered on the brink of independence since the 1870s. Huge quantities of ethnographical material flowed in during the late Victorian and Edwardian periods – the flotsam of empire turned into an anthropologist's dream. By 1967, ninety-five per cent of this material had to be stacked away in the basement. At last in 1970 the ethnographical collections were moved elsewhere, to Burlington Gardens, behind the Royal Academy. And the department's new home was a building worth waiting for: a grand palazzo originally built in 1866–9 as the London University Senate House [91]. Its architect was Sir James Pennethorne (1801–71), an R.I.B.A. Gold Medallist, for many years

91. British Museum Ethnography Department, Burlington Gardens,
Sir James Pennethorne

official architect to the Crown Estate and the author of numerous schemes for metropolitan improvement. Pennethorne's origins were mysterious – he was rumoured to be a child of George IV and John Nash's wife – but there was never any doubt about his talent. Like his brother John – an architectural archaeologist who anticipated Penrose's findings on the curvature of the Parthenon – he trained in Nash's office and travelled extensively abroad. He inherited to the full his master's facility of design and breadth of vision, and his best known work – the west wing of Somerset House – certainly matches up to the genius of Sir William Chambers. In Burlington Gardens Pennethorne's mastery of Cinquecento forms is complete. And his boldly modelled design, bristling with significant sculpture (twenty-two statues in all) amply qualifies as a suitable architectural adjunct to Britain's national museum.

And what of the library? Only the installation of sliding presses made possible its continued expansion in the 1880s. By 1910 there were 3,000,000 printed books on 46 miles of shelving. By 1950, additions were running at the rate of $1\frac{1}{4}$ miles of shelving each year. Today there must be well over 7 million volumes crammed along more than 80 miles of shelving. . . . And of the making of books there is no end. Panizzi's cuckoo has long since outgrown its Neo-classical nest.

What can be done about it? As early as 1823, Sir James Mackintosh recognized that a museum and a library are 'clean different things': the latter should be protected from intrusion, otherwise the student must be exposed to interruption. Far different was the case with a museum; for that, to be really useful, must be made an alluring lounge, to entice, as it were, the spectators to acquire, in the easiest way, a taste for the arts. Great Russell Street was rather out of the way for such a purpose. But one and a half centuries later the problem is still more easily recognized than solved. Put in its simplest terms, the conundrum runs as follows. A national museum knows only one law: expansion – a closed museum is a dead museum. But no architect has ever devised a single depository with a capacity for infinite growth. What, then, if the depositories are multiplied? Is decentralization possible without fragmentation? Well, that depends on the centre. And the centre of a capital city like London is an organism of mighty complexity. The problems of museology are as nothing to the problems of urbanization. Hence the cacophany of competing interests which have turned the expansion of the British Museum into one of the 'non-stop planning follies' of all time.

The battle of Bloomsbury really began in 1895. For in that year the Trustees – and the Exchequer – made their intentions plain by buying up the adjacent land on all four sides of the site: Great Russell Street to the south; Bloomsbury Street and Bedford Square to the west; Montague Place to the north; and Montague Street to the east. Sixty-nine houses were involved, and the price paid to the Bedford estate was £200,000. At last, it seemed, the museum had broken out of its shell. Expansion was in the air. A timely bequest of £50,000 from Vincent Stuckey Lean arrived in 1899. Four years later the Treasury authorized a grant of £150,000. And the architect commissioned was among the finest exponents of the British classical tradition, John James Burnet (1859–1938).

Burnet was a Glasgow man, educated at the École des Beaux Arts in Paris. And his work manages to combine the simplicity of the Glaswegian tradition with the flexibility of the Parisian. Burnet's museum extensions [92, 93, 94, 95] have been christened 'Greek Re-Revival'. But that

92. Scheme for extending the British Museum on all four sides (1905), J. J. Burnet

93. The Edward VII Galleries: original scheme (1905), J. J. Burnet

94. Scheme for extensions towards Bedford Square (1905), J. J. Burnet

is a metropolitan view. In Edwardian Glasgow the Greek Revival was still very much alive; and the Beaux Arts tradition was still a powerful force in architectural design. Only in London had Grecian been entirely superseded by Italianate. Burnet was not formally commissioned by the Trustees until 1903. He was chosen from a list of potential candidates drawn up by the R.I.B.A., after a preliminary scheme had been prepared by Henry Tanner (1849-1935), Taylor's successor at the Office of Works, best known as the architect of the Café Royal in Regent Street. But it

95. Scheme for the Edward VII Galleries and British Museum Avenue (1905), J. J. Burnet

seems a curious coincidence that in 1895 – the year of the museum's great leap forward – Burnet set out for the Continent and spent some months studying the conditions of museum design. Anyway, it was not until May 1914 that George V formally opened the Edward VII Galleries, and bestowed a knighthood on their architect.

The Edward VII Galleries to the north of the Round Reading Room marked a milestone in Burnet's career. Previously he had been a Caledonian master with Parisian proclivities. Now he was also the head of a big London firm. And his style became appropriately more eclectic. After the First World War, buildings in Aldwych, Kingsway, Oxford Street and Regent Street flowed from his office. But connoisseurs of late Victorian and Edwardian classicism – and there are now quite a number of them – prefer the purity of his Glasgow period – the former Fine Art Institute (1879-80) or the old Athenaeum (1886) – to the cosmopolitanism of his later work – Kodak House, Kingsway (1911), for example. In Bloomsbury Burnet's talent reached a state of happy equipoise – historicism mitigated by modernity – exactly half way through his architectural career. The R.I.B.A. Gold Medal followed, belatedly, in 1923.

Burnet's is an essentially synthetic design. There are echoes here of 'Greek' Thomson and Mackintosh, as well as memories of the Atelier Pascal. He set out to combine the scale and dignity of Smirke's work with the qualities of profile and finish which derive from modern materials. Grecian motifs, boldly adapted, supplied the medium – a means, not an end in themselves. 'The result', wrote W. H. Godfrey soon after Burnet's death, 'is by common consent one of the most important contributions to the architecture of this century. The great single order of twenty Ionic columns, between their flanking pylons, achieves the maximum of dignity and repose. The composition is much more than a brilliant exercise on a classic theme; every subtlety of varying diameter, intercolumniation, and inclination of verticals was employed to secure grace and homogeneity and it is justly acclaimed for its modern vigour and originality.' Burnet's 'subtle, voluminous and powerful building', writes Sir John Summerson, 'is directly in the tradition of Duc's Palais de Justice and Ginain's library at the École de Medicine. His colonnade is brilliantly handled – stretched like a screen from one massive pylon to another, overlapping the pylons at each end in such a way as to give the colonnade all the dignity of independence while relating it harmoniously to a building of fundamentally modern character.'

Unfortunately – like Smirke's section of the museum – Burnet's design has never been seen to full advantage. Its setting has been truncated and its sculptural decoration was never completed. 'British Museum Avenue', a short-lived vista along the line of Torrington Square [95], is now the site of Sir Charles Holden's bulky University Senate House. And Sir George Frampton's statues of Art and Science – designed to decorate Burnet's flanking pylons – were, like Westmacott's statues for the south front, never executed [93]. If sculpture is the voice of architecture, then the British Museum has whispered all its life.

The museum's new galleries formed part of a comprehensive plan [92]: exhibition and storage space on the northern and eastern sides of the site and a domed lecture theatre on the western side with a separate entrance from Bedford Square [94]. Even the great south front was to be extended, with wings abutting on Bloomsbury Street and Montague Street. But only the first stage of the project was executed: the galleries of British and Medieval Antiquities; the Print Room; the Map Room; and the North Library. The summer of 1914 was not a suitable season for building. But the sections which were built were built well. The gilded metalwork of the lift enclosure, executed by the Bromsgrove Guild, is a good example of the standard of workmanship involved. And though the new North Library had its critics – the *Museums Journal* compared it to 'a magnificent Nonconformist place of worship' – there was no denying its substantiality. Before it was 'modernized' by J. H. Markham (1883–1961) of the Office of Works, architect of the Geological Museum in South Kensington, it was certainly a convincing example of Edwardian gusto.

So Burnet's scheme survives merely as a torso, a museological dream cut short by the First World War. Still, enough remains to justify Goodhart-Rendel's judgement: Burnet was 'a Frenchified Scotsman, extraordinarily nice, with a tremendous love of order and system. He never lost hold of the essentials and thought no one in England knew anything about them. He used to say that nothing ought to be done without a decision behind it. He had no interest in style as such. . . . He really was a great man.'

The British Museum's expansion in the years before the First World War was accompanied by another piece of decentralization: the removal of newspapers from Bloomsbury to Colindale. The Colindale repository at Hendon in North London – half an hour's journey on the underground railway – was opened in 1903 as an overflow bookstack in debased Queen Anne Style. It was not until 1932 that a reading room was created there, together with an additional bookstore designed by J. H. Markham. The *Library Association Record* announced its pleasure at this 'striking structure in the modern style'. And consciences were perhaps reassured when the Bibliothèque Nationale followed suit in 1934 and transferred their newspapers from Paris to Versailles. But the move itself was a fateful one. Once dismemberment of the library had begun, where was the line to be drawn?

This was the sort of problem discussed at length by the Royal Commission on National Museums and Galleries, 1927–30. The new repository at Colindale formed part of the Commission's recommended building programme, prepared as an interim measure by Sir Richard Allinson (1869–1958), Tanner's successor at the Office of Works. He suggested, *inter alia*, the reconstruction of Sydney Smirke's Iron Library, quadrant by quadrant, so as to increase the accommodation for books. At the same time Lord Duveen (1869–1939) stepped forward as the patron the museum had been waiting for: the man to make possible the creation of a worthy setting for the Elgin Marbles. But some strange fate seemed to hang over Bloomsbury. The Edward VII Galleries had been completed in 1914; the Duveen Gallery was finished in 1939. And this time war meant not just the curtailment of the building programme, but the partial destruction of the new buildings themselves. The Duveen Gallery, built to designs by John Russell Pope of New York at a cost of £150,000, was shattered by bombs one night in 1940 – before the Elgin Marbles had even been installed. Worse still, the south-west quadrant of the Iron Library was destroyed in 1941, along with 250,000 books. The Elgin Marbles survived, safe and sound, sandbagged in a tube tunnel below London. More transportable items were hidden in a bomb-proof stone quarry far away from the capital. But the old storage block at Colindale was totally destroyed, with 30,000 newspaper volumes; the ceiling of Smirke's King's Library was blown apart by a high-explosive missile; the Medal Room, the Greek Bronze Room and the Greek and Roman Life Rooms were destroyed by incendiaries; and Burnet's Edward VII Galleries only escaped because, quite miraculously, two high-explosive bombs fell through the same aperture on different nights and both failed to explode.

However the impact of Hitler's blitz on the British Museum was far less devastating than it might have been. The real catastrophe of the second war – like the first – was the collapse of the museum's overall programme of expansion. The repair of war damage was slow enough – the Duveen Gallery [96] was not opened until 1962. But the revival of expansionist impetus was slower still. In effect, the museum had to re-fashion its plans all over again, for the third time in half a century. And this time the process of gestation took no less than twenty-five years – and almost ended in disaster.

It started in 1943. In that year discussions began which eventually produced the County of London Plan by Sir Patrick Abercrombie and J. H. Forshaw (1944), and Sir Patrick Abercrombie's Greater London Plan (1945). Both indicated expansion in the immediate neighbourhood. And

6. Inside the Duveen Gallery: the present home of the Elgin Marbles

in the Labour Government's Town and Country Planning Act of 1947 these indications were confirmed. Preservation of Leverton's Bedford Square was now recognized as essential. Burnet's scheme was therefore finally abandoned, and the area opposite the front of the British Museum, between Great Russell Street and New Oxford Street, was chosen instead as the new site for a new library. This vision of a Bloomsbury precinct was then incorporated – in the year of the Festival of Britain – in the London County Council's Greater London Development Plan (1951). In the following year a public inquiry was held. All went well, and in 1955-6 the plan was endorsed by the Tory Minister of Housing and Local Government after a debate in the House of Commons. Meanwhile the Trustees had come to the conclusion that the designated site might, in the long run, not be large enough for the whole library; and in 1959 they decided, with government backing, to create a new National Reference Library of Science and Invention on the South Bank of the Thames. This was to unite the museum's own scientific books, and those of the Patent Office Library. But the South Bank site never materialized, and scientific volumes were temporarily out-housed in Bayswater and Woolwich.

However, the Bloomsbury programme was by no means forgotten. Piece by piece, the Ministry of Works gradually bought up the various freeholds on the site, until three fifths of the land had been acquired at a cost of £2,000,000. In 1962 the Borough of Holborn agreed to co-operate, provided that domestic and commercial development was incorporated in the plan. And in August of that year the Tory Ministry of Works at last appointed two architects to prepare plans in consultation with a committee of the Trustees. The architects chosen were Sir Leslie Martin and Mr Colin St John Wilson, a partnership with considerable experience in town planning and library design. In September 1964 their scheme [97] was released to the press, after approval by the Trustees and the Ministry of Public Building and Works. It consisted of a multiple

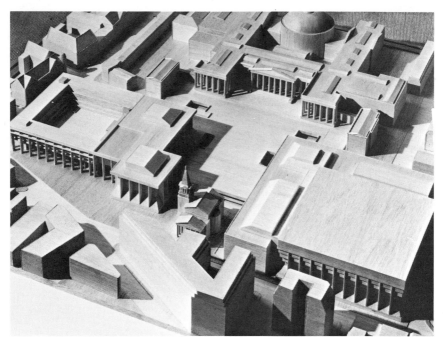

97. Plan for a new British Museum library (1964),
Sir Leslie Martin and Colin St John Wilson

development combining several related items: a central pedestrian
piazza stretching from the museum to Hawksmoor's St George's church,
with an underground car park below; a new library on the eastern side,
with seating for 1,100 readers in several rooms and 1,000,000 square feet
of storage space; a new lecture theatre, exhibition building and restaur-
ant on the western side; as well as twenty-one shops or offices and 106
housing units. It was scheduled to be built during the 1970s, at an estimated cost of £10,000,000.

Here at last was a scheme which would carry the British Museum into
the twenty-first century. The Departments of Antiquities, of Coins and
Medals and of Ethnography would stay in the old building. The Departments of Printed Books, of Manuscripts and of Prints and Drawings, as

well as the Copyright Office, would move across Great Russell Street
into a museologist's promised land. The King's Library would remain
intact, linked to the new reading rooms by underground passages. From
a town planner's point of view, the Martin–Wilson project fulfilled a
long-cherished ambition: the opening up of a grand vista from Hawksmoor's tower to Smirke's colonnade. This had been Nash's original
intention in the 1820s. This had been the dream of W. R. Lethaby (1857–
1931) just before the First World War [98]. This had been among the

98. A scheme for linking
the British Museum
and Waterloo Bridge (c. 1912),
W. R. Lethaby

main objects of half a dozen precinctual planning programmes during the 1940s and 1950s. And here was a design which really did justice to the site. Not just a tower block; not just a bookstack; but a majestically spacious composition, a worthy setting for two major historic monuments, Smirke's museum and Hawksmoor's church. Here was a complex of buildings, modern in finish and design, which managed – by a combination of broad horizontal massing and slim vertical emphases – to maintain the classical proportions of its environment. Here indeed, as Sir Frank Francis put it, was 'the opportunity of creating what may well be the building of the century and certainly the most up-to-date national library in the world'; a building worthy of one of the few British institutions known and respected, in Moscow, Washington, Buenos Aires or Tokyo.

The museum world held its breath. Was it really possible that the world's first national museum was about to take the lead again, for the first time since the death of Panizzi? The various departments involved began to prepare for removal. A government-sponsored Committee – the Parry Report on Libraries, 1967 – confidently referred to the prospect of a proper National Library. And then the bubble burst. On Friday 27 October 1967 *The Times* carried three black headlines on three different pages: 'No National Library in Bloomsbury' . . . 'An Unworthy Decision' . . . 'B.M. Trustees vent their wrath'. The London Borough of Camden – urged on by Mrs Lena Jeger, Labour M.P. for Holborn and St Pancras – had objected to the Martin–Wilson plan. And the objection had been upheld by the Labour Government's Secretary of State for Education and Science, Mr Patrick Gordon Walker, M.P. To him fell the privilege of announcing to a dumbfounded House of Commons that he had decided to abandon the Bloomsbury site: he had no other particular site in mind, but he intended to set up a National Libraries committee to find one.

The chorus of disapproval was deafening. Members of all three political parties united in condemnation of the decision as 'a national disgrace'.

After only a few months in office Mr Gordon Walker had thought fit to ignore not only the Standing Commission on Museums and Galleries, but the Trustees themselves – re-empowered by Act of Parliament as recently as 1963 to care for the nation's collections. Lord Radcliffe accused him of 'arrogance, . . . vanity, . . . ignorance, . . . almost unbelievable administrative incompetence, . . . constitutional impropriety . . . and . . . gross discourtesy'. Earl Jellicoe called the decision 'a monumental gaffe'. Lord Robbins thought it 'a gratuitous insult'. Lord Evans talked of cultural 'butchery'. Lord Snow sniffed collusion in the corridors of power. Lord Eccles spoke of 'technological dictators' throwing away one last chance – the chance 'to keep the whole conspectus of our culture on one site'. Sir Edward Boyle criticized Mr Gordon Walker's characteristically 'cavalier treatment of a statutory body'. Mr Geoffrey Rippon accused him of 'lying' about previous decisions in order to justify his own mistake. Lord Annan expressed his 'sense of outrage' at both the 'manner and content' of the decision. Its content had 'buried twenty years of planning'; and as for its manner, in Lord Radcliffe's phrase, all talk of 'consultation' was no more than 'a travesty of language'. Lord Concsford concluded that this 'sense of outrage' was 'shared by every educated man'. The Trustees publicly announced that they would risk dismissal by Act of Parliament rather than agree to the dismemberment of their collections – the very reversal of the museum's articles of foundation. Scholars from all over the world likened the threat of breaking up the British Museum to the dissolution of the ancient library at Alexandria. As for the new Committee, *The Times* dismissed it as 'a piece of Whitehall flannel'.

Mr Gordon Walker's decision was certainly shot through with absurdities. His action had supposedly been prompted by the housing needs of the Borough of Camden. Yet the chairman of Camden's Planning and Development Committee declared that he was almost as surprised as the Trustees by the timing of the decision, and was in fact prepared to negotiate. The decision was supposedly substantiated by the initiation of a full-scale inquiry into the country's library facilities. But when the membership of the new National Libraries Committee (the Dainton Committee) was announced, it was found to contain not even one librarian. In effect, only three arguments were produced in support of Mr Gordon Walker's action. All three were quickly exposed as absurdities.

In the first place it was argued that the rehousing of 900 residents would be both difficult and unjust. That was emotive nonsense. The Martin–Wilson plan provided accommodation for more than 300, and the number could have been increased. Thousands of Londoners were being rehoused each year because of road and redevelopment schemes. Anyway the numbers involved were small compared with the number of visitors to the British Museum – currently more than 1,800,000 per year. And where else in central London was there a site equally convenient for scholars and visitors alike, and equally underpopulated? In the second place it was argued that the great, central copyright library was a thing of the past: the future lay with smaller specialist libraries, linked by electronic devices. That was academic nonsense. During the nineteenth century, as specialism increased, scholastic disciplines moved further apart, to their own mutual detriment. During the twentieth century this process of fragmentation has been reversed, and as the various disciplines move closer towards a new synthesis research has become increasingly interdisciplinary. As for electronics making geographical considerations irrelevant, even the most advanced computer has yet to equal the flexibility of the printed page. In the third place it was argued that the rejection of the Martin–Wilson plan would mean the preservation of an historic and 'fascinating' part of London. That was sentimental nonsense. The chairman of the Labour party's own arts group dismissed the area as 'a dog's dinner'. The designated area contained only one building of any aesthetic significance, Nash's Pharmaceutical Society headquarters. And so far from pressing for the preservation of their building, the pharmacists had already commissioned an architect to design a new one.

Why then was the decision taken? As Lord Eccles later remarked, 'we shall never know exactly why'. Perhaps it was merely a combination of economy and procrastination. Within weeks of supporting the decision, the Prime Minister announced the devaluation of the pound. As the Labour Government slithered to an unprecedented series of by-election disasters, 'austerity thinking' seemed to preclude a £10,000,000 investment in 'culture'. Perhaps it was simply an instance of local political pressure – Bloomsbury's promised land had been turned into Naboth's vineyard. Almost the only person who publicly rejoiced at the decision was the local M.P., Mrs Lena Jeger. She blithely told the House of Commons that the proposed piazza was no more than 'a draughty great yard'. An architect of genius, Mr Ove Arup, thought differently: he accused the government of conspiring 'to strangle a masterpiece at birth'. All in all it seems that two misguided politicians joined forces to secure the triumph of philistinism over imagination and common sense.

Happily their triumph was ephemeral and empty of political reward. Within months of his announcement Mr Gordon Walker was back among the back-benchers. After a dismal series of ministerial jobs, he retired from active politics. Having nearly ruined Britain's national library, he was put in charge of the reorganization of the English alphabet. It would have been pure farce, had it not been pure tragedy. But the final irony was still to come. The new National Libraries Committee was given a fairly open brief:

To examine the functions and organization of the British Museum Library, the National Central Library, the National Lending Library for Science and Technology and the Science Museum Library in providing national library facilities; to consider whether in the interests of efficiency and economy such facilities should be brought into a unified framework; and to make recommendations.

Only one recommendation was barred: that the National Library should be built on the Bloomsbury site. After more than a year's investigation, after spending £26,523 on the production of a 335-page report, that was precisely the recommendation arrived at: 'Geographical separation of the library departments of the British Museum from the antiquities departments would not have advantages for staff or visitors nor would it assist the creation of a national libraries service. From library considerations alone, therefore, the Bloomsbury site is the most suitable.'

The other recommendations of the Dainton Report were equally predictable: the British Museum Library should change its title to the National Reference Library; its sub-section, the National Reference Library of Science and Invention, should be known as the Central Science and Patent Collections; the two national lending libraries, the National Central Library and the National Lending Library for Science and Technology, should both be based outside London, at Boston Spa, Yorkshire; bibliographical services should be properly coordinated by the British National Bibliography; and all five of these organizations should be governed by a new statutory body, the National Libraries Authority. The Science Museum Library was to remain outside this mighty network, to serve the needs of Imperial College. What did it all amount to? *The Times* delivered yet another broadside. The Dainton Committee had merely raised the spectre of a new 'Bureaucracy of Books'. The physical future of the British Museum remained unresolved. And the Labour Government's notorious decision remained 'a crass blunder'.

But rescue was not far off. At last, in March 1970, came the dénouement. A discreet eight months after the appearance of the Dainton Report, an astute forty-eight hours before the Greater London Council elections, the Labour Government announced its conversion. The proposed administrative reorganization was endorsed *en bloc*. And the site of the new library was to be in Bloomsbury after all. The integrity of the museum was to be preserved. The Trustees hailed the decision as 'a victory for commonsense'. The Cabinet had at least had the courage to change its collective mind. So the architects unrolled their plans once more. But this time they faced a more difficult challenge. The site (or battlefield) to the south of Great Russell Street was now restricted by the need to preserve Bloomsbury Square – including Nash's Pharmaceutical Society. And this narrower site was to be made to carry an even higher density of building. The four sections of the National Reference Library for Science and Invention were to be united on the same site with the new National Reference Library. And the proportion of housing was to be significantly increased. Still, it was a challenge worth taking up. The extra pressure on the new site might even allow the continued use of the Round Reading Room. In the House of Lords, Lord Eccles expressed 'the great relief and warm thanks' of all the Trustees. Work could now begin, he announced, on a complex of museum buildings which would be the envy of all nations and 'without equal in Europe or America'. Early in 1971 a new Tory government – with Lord Eccles now Minister responsible for the Arts – announced its general endorsement of the grand design. The new 'Bureaucracy of Books', however, was to be called the British Library. And the estimated cost had now jumped to £36,000,000.

Meanwhile work began on an interim 'amenities block'. Designed by Mr Colin St John Wilson, this comprised a gallery for temporary exhibitions; new restaurants for public and staff; space for educational services; a display gallery for coins and medals; and improved office accommodation. Its location was the last vacant area on the old museum site behind Smirke's western wing. In other words, Taylor's White Wing was now to be balanced, as inconspicuously as possible, by a modest modern block.

As the British Museum moves into the 1970s, its architectural problems remain unique. It is a research institute, a museum and a library rolled into one. Frenchmen marvel at the way it combines half the Louvre with the whole of the Bibliothèque Nationale. Russians wonder at its conjunction of the Lenin Library with the Russian Historical

Museum. Americans regret that in their case Joel Barlow's unitary visions in the early nineteenth century were not fulfilled: in Washington expensive links have now to be forged between the Smithsonian Institution, its neighbouring universities and the Library of Congress. Only Bloomsbury enables scholars to study civilization in the round: printed and unprinted records, plus significant artefacts. No wonder, during the summer months, nearly half the scholars in the reading room come from abroad. This unique contiguity – books, manuscripts and works of art – must surely be preserved at all costs, despite the arguments of the fragmenters. During the great debate of autumn 1967, there was a good deal of centrifugal reasoning in the air. Fears were raised that whole sections of the museum might be banished 'to Potters Bar or Birmingham'. 'How should we like to visit the Bibliothèque Nationale in Ivry-sur-Seine', wrote one correspondent to *The Times*, 'or the Library of Congress in Richmond, Virginia? Anybody who has trekked from the Metropolitan Museum to the Cloisters (mid Central Park to the uttermost tip of Manhattan) . . . knows the answer to that one.'

No, Bloomsbury – 'London's doormat' – is more accessible than Birmingham or York. Bloomsbury is the place for Britain's national museum *and* Britain's national library. But quite clearly the British Museum of the twenty-first century will be rather different to the one we used to know. Libraries are fast becoming laboratories geared to maximum 'information retrieval'. Panizzi's poor student now expects carrels, microfilm, microfiche, microcard, film projectors, tape, record booths, conveyor belts and telex as well as computerized bibliographies. And in the fields of conservation and restoration, in the scientific analysis of works of art, vast strides are being made. But museums are not only becoming more mechanized. They are becoming more hospitable. Their emphasis is shifting from research to education, from the extension of knowledge to its diffusion, from the maintenance of standards to a kind of cultural evangelism. In the true sense of the word the business of museums has emerged as amusement. Conservation, ventilation, storage, transportation, parking facilities, conference centres, cloakrooms, restaurants, public relations departments, departmental libraries, cinemas, bookstalls, lecture rooms – the services are starting to overwhelm the collections. The trivia seem to be driving out the treasures. In the new Israeli Museum in Jerusalem offices occupy two thirds of the total space, and galleries one third. The reconstructed Palazzo Reale di Capodimonte in Naples is memorable not only for its exquisite Neoclassical decor, but for the prodigious electronics system which that decoration conceals. Technology and mass education have together transformed museology. And the architect – society's midwife – has to make the whole thing possible.

It was easier a hundred years ago. In 1875 when critics talked of popularizing Britain's greatest museum, the Rev. J. P. Mercier supplied the official answer:

The British Museum . . . is not a place of pleasant resort, or for recreation joined to elegant instruction and amusement, like the South Kensington [Victoria and Albert] Museum. It is a solemn, serious place, and as heavy in its deportment and general character as the ponderous relics of antiquity which it contains. It is a veritable mummified affair, unenlivened except by the swarms of dirty children who are sent there to pass the time while their mothers are out charing, and who frequently play at hide and seek among the deities of ancient Egypt or Assyria . . . [Most of the collections are merely] 'caviare to the general'. As National property, it must be . . . open freely to the public . . . But it is essentially the resort of scholars, and of the learned and the scientific. Few others can understand or appreciate it; nor will any amount of learning and sermonising make them do so.

Not surprisingly, public lectures were not introduced at the British Museum until 1911.

But five years before Mercier's reactionary statement, America's leading museum had struck a very different note. The 1870 programme of the Metropolitan Museum of Art announced that its purpose was to offer 'to our whole people free and ample means for innocent and refined enjoyment, and also . . . the best facilities for practical instruction and for the cultivation of pure taste in all matters connected with the arts.' *Mutatis mutandis*, and discounting the concept of 'pure taste', that is the programme of most modern museums. There is a new audience now, and they want a different sort of show.

As the world's first national museum, the British Museum has been perhaps a little slow to adapt itself to the new situation. But in 1969 the opening of fourteen new Greek and Roman galleries [99] fully confirmed its capacity for change. Designed for the Ministry of Public Building and Works by Mr Robin Wade, on the advice of Professors R. D. Russell and R. Y. Goodden, these new rooms combine utility and drama, atmosphere and practicality. So do the new Assyrian Galleries opened in 1970 [100]. In all these new galleries the arrangement is chronological and selective, based on the principle of separating primary and secondary material: secondary galleries for research; primary galleries, containing top-quality exhibits, simply arranged to appeal to a wide audience. The Smirke interiors have been rendered less emphatic, their walls masked and their coffered ceilings stripped of all polychromy. One piece of luck contributed greatly to the final result. The haphazard growth of the gallery layout on the building's western side during the early Victorian period had accidentally produced a single striking advantage: the sequence of rooms was nicely varied in shape and size. The new galleries make the most of this inherited variety and at the same time manage to impose an element of coherence by the use of standard surfaces and uniform fittings. Only the strident ochre floor-tiling detracts from the integrity and harmony of the whole design.

Through these new galleries the spectator is guided, gently but firmly, from one delight to another; and, as he goes, he is informed about what he sees, without being overwhelmed by the volume of information.

99. The Nereid Monument in the new Greek and Roman galleries (1969)

100. The Khorsobad Bulls in the new Assyrian galleries (1970)

Occasionally the impact is electrifying. Several key exhibits – the gigantic Khorsobad bulls, the Payava tomb, the reconstituted Nereid monument, the unbroken Bassae frieze and Elgin's solitary caryatid from the Erechtheion – are now presented more excitingly than ever before, visible from all angles and instantly comprehensible. Away with *auguste ennui*. The spirit of Santayana's dictum is omnipresent: 'beauty is objectified pleasure.' Here past and present mingle happily. Here, walking in these new galleries, the future of the British Museum seems secure.

Bibliography

Note: The place of publication is London unless otherwise stated.

I: THE IDEA OF A MUSEUM

G. Bazin, *The Museum Age*, 1967, is the most recent history of museology, comprehensive and well-illustrated. Certain aspects are dealt with in a more detailed and scholarly manner in V. Plagemann, *Das Deutsche Kunstmuseum, 1790–1870,* Munich 1969: Sir F. Kenyon, *Libraries and Museums*, 1930, covers the whole field with remarkable brevity and no pictures. E. Edwards, *Memoirs of Libraries,* 2 vols., 1859, W. H. Flower, *Essays on Museums*, 1898, and D. Murray, *Museums: their History and their Use*, 3 vols., 1904, all contain a good deal of recondite information. So does F. H. Taylor, *The Taste of Angels*, 1948, though in rather more palatable form and not always reliable. J. W. Clark, *The Care of Books,* 1902, deals with medieval and Renaissance libraries; so does C. and M. Elton, *The Great Book Collectors,* 1893. Alma S. Wittlin, *The Museum: its History and its Tasks in Education*, 1949, only partly succeeds in explaining the development of museums in psychological and sociological terms. R. C. Smith, *A Bibliography of Museums and Museum Work,* Washington, 1928, is a valuable research tool. Recent work on the architectural origins of the museum is discussed in H. Huth, 'Museum and Gallery', in O. Goetz (ed.), *Essays in Honour of G. Swarzenski,* Chicago, 1951, pp. 238-44 and H. Seling, 'The Genesis of the Museum', *Architectural Review*, cxli, 1967, pp. 103–14.

2: THE OLD BRITISH MUSEUM

E. Edwards, *Lives of the Founders of the British Museum, 1570–1870,* 1890, is a mine of information, ponderous but invaluable. H. C. Shelley, *The British Museum,* Boston, 1911, covers much the same ground in a bright and breezy way. The standard biography of Dr Sloane is Sir G. R. De Beer, *Sir Hans Sloane and the British Museum,* 1953. Descriptions of Montagu House are contained in J. Britton and A. C. Pugin, *Public Buildings of London*, i, 1825, E. Walford, *Old and New London*, iv, 1883-4, and I Dunlop, 'The First Home of the British Museum',

Country Life, cx (1951), pp. 812–14. J. Harris discusses the schemes of Cornelius Johnston and John Vardy in *Apollo*, August 1969. Plans by Sir Christopher Wren and William Kent for re-housing the Cottonian Collection are described and illustrated in *Wren Society*, xi, 1934, pp. 48–59. Ralph Montagu's building operations at Boughton and elsewhere are analysed by J. Cornforth in *Country Life*, cxlviii (1970), pp. 564–8, 624–8, 684–7. E. Croft-Murray's *Decorative Painting in England, 1537–1837*, 1962, supplies documentary details for the painted rooms of Montagu House. The topographical history of the area is dealt with in detail by Eliza Jeffries Davis in 'The University Site, Bloomsbury', *London Topographical Record*, xvii, 1926, pp. 19–139. And contemporary French influence on English architecture is discussed by G. Jackson-Stops in *Country Life*, cxlvii, 1970, pp. 261–6.

3: SIR ROBERT SMIRKE AND THE GREEK REVIVAL

Sections of this chapter have been adapted from J. Mordaunt Crook, 'Architect of the Rectangular: a Reassessment of Sir Robert Smirke', *Country Life*, cxli, 1967, pp. 846–8; 'Sir Robert Smirke: a Centenary Florilegium', *Architectural Review*, cxlii, 1967, pp. 208–10; 'A Vanished Theatrical Masterpiece: Smirke's Covent Garden Theatre', *Country Life Annual*, 1970, pp. 102–5; 'Sir Robert Smirke: a Regency Architect in London', *Journal of the London Society*, no. 381 (March 1968), pp. 2–11; and 'The Career of Sir Robert Smirke, R.A.' (D.Phil., Oxford, 1961). H. Honour, *Neo-classicism*, 1968, is the best general discussion of the Neo-classical movement. Its architectural aspects are surveyed in four general works: Sir Albert Richardson, *Monumental Classic Architecture in Great Britain and Ireland during the 18th and 19th Centuries*, 1914, Sir John Summerson, *Architecture in Britain, 1530–1830*, 1969 ed., H. R. Hitchcock, *Architecture: Nineteenth and Twentieth Centuries*, 1968 ed.; J. Mordaunt Crook, *The Greek Revival: Neo-Classical Attitudes in British Architecture, 1760–1870* (in the press); and in two monographs: D. Watkin, *Thomas Hope and the Neo-Classical Idea*, 1968, and Dora Wiebenson, *Sources of Greek Revival Architecture*, 1969.

Regency archaeology, tourism and connoisseurship are dealt with in H. Levin, *The Broken Column*, 1931, T. Spencer, *Fair Greece, Sad Relic*, 1954, W. St Clair, *Lord Elgin and the Marbles*, 1967 and B. Fothergill, *Sir William Hamilton*, 1969. The standard history of the Society of Dilettanti is L. Cust and S. Colvin, *The History of the Society of Dilettanti*, 1898. The theoretical premises of Neo-classicism are provocatively discussed in E. Kauffman, *Architecture in the Age of Reason*,

1955, and P. Collins, *Changing Ideals in Modern Architecture, 1750-1950*, 1965. Parallels between Neo-classical architecture, sculpture and painting are analysed in H. Hawley, *Neo-Classicism, Style and Motif*, 1964, D. Irwin, *English Neo-Classical Art*, 1966, and R. Rosenblum, *Transformations in 18th Century Art*, Princeton, N.J., 1967.

For the Greek Revival in Scotland see A. J. Youngson, *The Making of Classical Edinburgh* (1966) and A. Gomme and D. Walker, *The Architecture of Glasgow* (1968).

For transatlantic parallels see T. Hamlin, *Greek Revival Architecture in America* (1944).

4: THE NEW BRITISH MUSEUM

Sections of this chapter have been adapted from a fully documented account of the museum's rebuilding in J. Mordaunt Crook and M. H. Port, *The History of the King's Works, vol. v, 1782-1852*, ed. H. M. Colvin (to be published by H.M.S.O.). This will supersede Sir F. Kenyon, *The Building of the British Museum*, 1914. An article by Sir Nikolaus Pevsner, 'The British Museum, 1753-1953', *Architectural Review*, cxiii, 1953, pp. 179-82, contains an ingenious but inaccurate explanation of the genesis of Sir Robert Smirke's design. Several visionary French precedents are illustrated in Helen Rosenau (ed.), 'The Engravings of the Grands Prix of the French Academy of Architecture', *Architectural History*, iii, 1960. Smirke's structural techniques are discussed in J. Mordaunt Crook, 'Sir Robert Smirke: a Pioneer of Concrete Construction', *Transactions of the New-comen Society*, xxxviii, 1965-6, pp. 5-22. See also S. B. Hamilton, 'Old Cast-Iron Structures', *The Structural Engineer*, xxvii, 1949, pp. 173-91 and xxviii, 1950, pp. 79-81 and H. J. Gough, 'Tests on Cast-Iron Girders Removed from the British Museum', *Institution of Civil Engineers, Selected Engineering Papers*, no. 161, 1934.

5: THE ROUND READING ROOM

There are several biographies of Sir Anthony Panizzi, notably those by L. A. Fagan, 2 vols., 1880, R. Cowtan, 1873, and Constance Brooks, 1931. The most recent is: E. Miller, *Prince of Librarians: Sir Anthony Panizzi*, 1967. The history of the British Museum library is dealt with entertainingly in R. Cowtan, *Memories of the British Museum*, 1872 and G. F. Barwick, *The Reading Room of the British Museum*, 1929, and rather more academically in A. J. K. Esdaile, *The British Museum Library*, 1948 ed. The development of public and national libraries in Britain and abroad was first surveyed by E. Edwards, *Public Libraries in London and Paris,* 1847, and J. W. and W. Papworth, *Museums, Libraries and Picture Galleries,* 1853. A. J. K. Esdaile, *National Libraries of the World,* 1957, and W. A. Munford, *Edward Edwards,* 1963, contain more recent studies of the same subject. Comparative plans of British libraries designed immediately before and after the First World War are included in W. A. Briscoe, *Library Planning,* 1927. For Sydney Smirke's architectural career, see J. Mordaunt Crook, 'Sydney Smirke', in *Seven Victorian Architects,* ed. Sir Nikolaus Pevsner (in the press); for Alfred Stevens, see K. Towndrow, *Alfred Stevens,* 1939; H. Stannus, *Alfred Stevens,* 1891, and Susan McMorran, 'Alfred Stevens', *R.I.B.A. Journal,* lxxi, 1964, pp. 435–40.

6: CRISIS

Early guide books to the Natural History Museum describe Waterhouse's buildings in some detail. There are two biographies of Sir William Flower, by C. J. Cornish, 1904, and R. Lydekker, 1906. The broadening of museological interests, to include industry and industrial art, is traced in C. R. Richards, *The Industrial Museum*, New York, 1925, and *Industrial Art and the Museum*, 1927.

Successive stages in the expansion of the Bloomsbury site are traced in Sir F. Kenyon, 'The British Museum: its Material Needs', *The Nineteenth Century,* xcvi, 1924, pp. 709–18. Burnet's architectural career is summarized in A. Gomme and D. Walker, *The Architecture of Glasgow,* 1968. New problems facing the museum are discussed by Sir F. Francis in 'The British Museum in Recent Times', *Librarianship and Literature: essays in honour of Jack Pafford,* ed. A. Taylor Milne, 1970. But the most recent crisis in the museum's history is best traced in the well-indexed files of *The Times* during the 1960s; in successive *Reports of the Trustees of the British Museum* over the same period; in the 'Dainton Report', i.e. the *Report of the National Libraries Committee* (H.M.S.O., 1969); and in *The British Library* (H.M.S.O., 1970: command paper 4572).

Recent trends in American museum and library design are summarized in T. Hamlin, ed., *Forms and Functions of 20th Century Architecture*, iii, 1952, pp. 675–750. The growth and organization of American museums is dealt with in detail in

L. V. Coleman, *Manual for Small Museums,* 1927, and *The Museum in America,* 3 vols., Washington, 1939, and in W. Pack, *The Art Museum in America,* New York, 1948. The purpose and value of museums in modern society is discussed in B. I. Gilman, *Museum Ideals of Purpose and Method,* Cambridge, Mass., 1918; Sir F. Kenyon, *Museums and National Life,* 1927; T. R. Adam, *The Civic Value of Museums,* New York, 1937, and *The Museum and Popular Culture,* New York, 1939; Eleanor M. Moore, *Youth in Museums,* Philadelphia, 1941; and T. L. Low, *The Museum as a Social Investment,* New York, 1942.

The new Greek and Roman galleries at the British Museum are illustrated and described in the *Architectural Review,* cxlvi, 1969, pp. 439-43.

Index

Kinfauns Castle, Perthshire, 84
Kinmount House, Dumfriesshire, 102
Klenze, Leo von, 107, 113, 119
Knight, Gowan, 157
Knight, R. Payne, 69, 71, 108-9
Korb, Hermann, 166

Laborde, Count Leon de, 166, 168, 208
Labrouste, Henri, 174, 192
Lafosse, Charles de, 58
Lamb, Charles, 61, 85
Lanchester, Lucas, and Lodge, Messrs, 192
Lansdowne, William, 1st Marquess of, 67, 76
Latrobe, B. H., 88
Laugier, M. A., 98, 99-101
Lawrence, Sir Thomas, 79, 108
Layard, Sir Henry, 197
Lean, V. Stuckey, 211
Le Brun, Charles, 58
Leeds, Brotherton Library, 191
Leeds, W. H., 172, 181
Leheup, Peter, 48
Lemercier, Jacques, 58, 60
Lenoir, Alexandre, 34
Leo X, Pope, 24
Le Pautre, Antoine, 61
Le Roy, J. D., 86-7
Lethaby, W. R., 221
Leverton, Thomas, 219
Lewes, Fitzroy Museum and Library, 203
Linnaeus (Karl von Linné), 44
Liverpool, Picton Reading Room, 191
Liverpool, Robert, 2nd Earl of, 77, 148
Locke, John, 191

LONDON
    Arundel House, 27, [29]; Ashburnham
    House, 41; Athenaeum Club, 81; Bank-
    ruptcy Courts, Carey Street, 199; Ban-
    queting House, Whitehall, 130; Bedlam
    Hospital, 56; Bloomsbury Place 44,
    Square 44, 46, 227, Street 211, 215;

Bow Street Police Station, 199; Buckingham House (old) 51, 130, library of 166,
[72]; Buckingham Palace, 78, 134, 141;
Burlington House, 108; Café Royal,
Piccadilly, 212; Carlton Club, 81, 82,
186; Carlton House, 77, 109, 129; Charing Cross Station, 186; Coal Exchange,
173, [77]; Cockpit, Whitehall, 55;
Colosseum, Regent's Park, 172; Conservative Club, 82, 186; Cotton House,
Westminster, 41; County Council, 219;
Covent Garden Theatre, 81, 102, 150,
[27]; Crystal Palace, 174, 176; Custom
House, 84, 103, 142-3; Essex House, 41;
Foreign Office, 190; General Post Office,
78, 103, 118, 120, 126; Geological Museum, South Kensington, 215; Hungerford Market, 174; Inner Temple, 75, 78,
85; King's College, 78, 103, 170, 179;
Kodak House, Kingsway, 214; Liverpool
Street Station, 175; London Bridge
Approaches, 75, 78-9; Mansion House,
41; Marlborough House, 199; Millbank
Penitentiary, 78, 84, 139; Montagu House,
see British Museum (old); National
Gallery, 94, [37], 129, 170, 172, 176, 199,
208; Natural History Museum, South
Kensington, see British Museum; Oxford
and Cambridge Club, 82; Patent Office,
199, library 219; Paddington Station,
175, 186; Pharmaceutical Society,
Bloomsbury Square, 224, 227; Public/
National Record Office, 117, 172, 191,
199; Royal College of Physicians (Canada
House), 82, 110, [29]; Royal College of
Surgeons, 58, 63; Royal Mint, 75, 78, 81;
St Anne, Wandsworth, 104; St George,
Bloomsbury, 60, 168, 220; St James,
West Hackney, 104; St James's Palace,
56, 77, Queen's Library 40; St Mary,
Bryanston Square, 104; St Martin-in-the-
Fields, 99; St Mary-le-Strand, 99; St
Paul's Cathedral, 40, 140, 145, 181, 188,

Oglander, Sir John, 37
Onslow, Arthur, 41-2, 48-9
Owen, Richard, 199
Oxford, Ashmolean Museum (old), 34, 36-8, 63, [10]; Ashmolean Museum (new), 38, 92, [33]; Bodleian Library, 36, 61; Oxford Museum, 200-201, [88]; Pitt Rivers Museum, 38; Radcliffe Camera, 166, [69]; Science Museum, 38; University, 36, 38, 48
Oxford, Edward, 5th Earl of, 79
Oxford, Henrietta, Dowager Countess of, 42

Paley, Dr, 63
Palladio, Andrea, 98
Panizzi, Sir Anthony, 155, 157-63, 168, 175-81, 187, 192-3, 195, 210, 222, 228, [68]
Papworth, John, 172
Papworth, Wyatt, 172
Paris, Bibliothèque Nationale, 159, 163, 192, 216, 227-8, [87]; Bibliothèque Sainte Geneviève, 174, [78]; Bourse, 149; École des Beaux Arts, 211, 212; École Royale, 32; Invalides, 58; Louvre, 32, 34, 168, 208, 227, Grande Galerie of 26, 28, [5], [6]; Madeleine, 149; Mazarine Palace, 168; Palais du Luxembourg, 32; Royal Academy, 48; Royal Library, 143, 159, 161, 162, 166, 168, 208, projects for [73], [74], [75]; Sainte Chapelle, 22; Tuileries, 28, 56, 60, 168
Parke, Robert, 113
Parker, Archbishop, 40
Parmentier, J., 58-9
Pasley, C. W., 141
Paty, Matthew, 157-8
Paxton, Sir Joseph, 170, 174
Peacock, H. S., 196-7
Pearce, Sir E. Lovett, 113
Pearce, J. A. H., 208
Peel, Sir Robert, 81, 115, 136, 138, 148, 208

Pelham, Henry, 48
Pennethorne, Sir James, 191, 199, 208, 210
Pennethorne, John, 210
Penrose, F. C., 210
Pergamum, 19-20
Perkins, 142
Perrault, Claude, 60
Perth, County Buildings, 76, 82
Peter the Great, of Russia, 36
Pevsner, Sir Nikolaus, 113
Philip II, of Spain, 27
Piranesi, G. B., 97
Pistol, 108
Pitt, William, 79, 81
Planché, J. Robinson, 79
Planta, Sir Joseph, 68, 109, 157-8
Playfair, W. H., 88, 93
Plutarch, 21
Pocoke, Richard, 86
Pontifex, 182
Ponton and Foster, Messrs, 203
Pope, Alexander, 46, 48, 191
Pope, J. Russell, 217
Porden, William, 77
Portland, Margaret, Duchess of, 42, 108
Powis, Edward, 6th Earl of, 81
Preston, Lanarkshire, 91; Harris Free Library, Museum, and Art Gallery, 94, [36]
Price and Manby, Messrs, 142
Priene, Temple of Athena Polias, 120, 150, [53], [54]
Prosser, Thomas, 175
Ptolemy Philadelphus, 19
Puckler-Muskau, Prince, 71
Puget, Pierre, 56
Pugin, A. W. N., 142, 148-149

Queensbury, Charles, 6th Marquess of, 76
Quicheberg, Samuel van, 63

Radcliffe, Cyril, 1st Viscount, 223
Rameses II, 21
Raphael, 24